Hand Drawn Illustrations
By
Bryony Grace Dorgan

Copyright © 2012 Kerri Formoso. All rights reserved

About the Author

Kerri Formoso is a Clinical Hypnotherapist with a busy practice on the outskirts of Bristol. She completed her training at The Clifton Practice (www.cpht.co.uk), one of the foremost Hypnotherapy training centres in the UK. Kerri holds a Hypnotherapy Practitioners Diploma, a nationally recognised hypnotherapy qualification endorsed by the Open University, as well as a Diploma in Hypnotherapy and Psychotherapy. She is a registered member of the National Council for Hypnotherapy (www.hypnotherapists.org.uk) and a member of the Association for Solution Focused Hypnotherapy (www.AfSFH.com). She is also registered on the Complementary and Natural Healthcare Council (www.cnhc.org.uk) register.

Kerri has appeared on both Heart FM radio and BBC Radio Bristol sharing her knowledge of hypnotherapy and solution focused therapy and has published articles in the Association for Solution Focused Hypnotherapy magazine and This Is Bristol, the online partner for the Bristol Evening Post.

In addition to her work as a hypnotherapist Kerri has a keen interest in the fields of neuroscience, epigenetics, quantum physics and the movement of modern science towards understanding spirituality and the associated brain activity.

For full details of her practice and more information about Kerri visit www.downendhypnotherapy.co.uk.

The Big Book of Metaphors

Acknowledgements

First and foremost to:

Cleo, Jeri, Maxine, Lewis and Bryony

It may have appeared over the years that I was teaching you,
But the truth is; it was always all of you teaching me.

I've learned more about life from all of you than I could ever have taught.

I'm so proud of all five of you,
You truly are incredible people to know.

To the rest of my family and friends:

I took an unexpected turn in the path and have been lucky enough to have you all with me when the Sat Nav wasn't there! For that I thank you; you have helped and supported me while I got my new bearings.

The Big Book of Metaphors

INDEX

	Introduction	9
1.	Clearing Problems To Find Solutions	17
	A Perfect Garden Metaphor	23
2.	Character Types	27
	Accepting What You Get Metaphor	31
3.	Procrastination	35
	Bus Stops Metaphor	39
4.	Weight Loss	41
	Clapped Out Car Metaphor	47
5.	Mirror Neurons	49
	Director of Happiness Metaphor	55
6.	Brain Wave Activity	59
	Facebook Timeline Metaphor	65
7.	Insomnia	69
	Fast Forward Metaphor	75
8.	Solution Focused Therapy	79
	Google Brain Metaphor	85
9.	Fears and Phobias	89
	New Film Metaphor	95
10.	Reticular Activating System	99
	Purple Shoes/Tie Metaphor	103
11.	Accepting Difficult Characters	107
	Rough Puff Pastry Metaphor	113
12.	Relationships & Neuroplasticity	115
	Sour Milk Metaphor	119
13.	Planning to Achieve	121
	SS Great Britain Metaphor	125
14.	Pregnancy	129
	Sticky Buds Metaphor	133
15.	Migraine	137

	Storm Control Metaphor	143
16.	Strong Willed Clients	147
	Tetris Metaphor	153
17.	Anxiety and Panic Attacks	157
	The Gift Metaphor	163
18.	Irritable Bowel Syndrome	165
	The Lock Keeper	171
19.	The Miracle Question	173
	Timeline Metaphor	177
20.	Letting Go Of A Relationship	179
	Vegetable Garden Metaphor	183
	Conclusion	187

The Big Book of Metaphors

Foreword

"Could you recommend a reading list?"

I am so lucky to be able to interact with students and graduates in the profession I very much care for. It is the inevitable consequence of being experienced; some people might say old, that I am asked questions. More often than not I can be helpful and, like all of us, I enjoy being helpful. In reply to the questions above though, I have always floundered a bit. This is perhaps surprising as I know I am a compulsive book buyer, although I do it more in hope than judgement. I am on record, and, I am not the only one, as saying that most books turn out to be a disappointment. I think only a small number of the books I have in my bookcase have been really worth reading. Worse, some are misleading and confusing.

I have always endeavoured to abide by what Dr James Braid said. He was adamant that the psychotherapists way should be 'up to date' and they should take note of the very best shown to us by experiences, literacy, research and science. Sadly finding the 'best' is easier said than done.

You can begin to see therefore having read Kerri's book, why I am cheered because I would have no hesitation in recommending 'The Big Book of Metaphors' to you. It is innovative, beautifully creative and adheres to the modern way of thinking.

I remember seeing Erickson (the DVD) for the first time. There were many things that stuck in my mind but perhaps the most pertinent comment of all came from one of his daughters in law. She was completing her degree course and asked her Father-in-law for help with quite severe examination nerves. As the treatment progressed she very much wanted to ask Erickson the question 'When are you going to address the problem?' In her words the sessions were always the same, "Dr Erickson started by saying "I know someone who.......and then told me a story". Needless to say there was a happy ending; Erickson's non-directive methods have recently been verified by the work of Rock and Schwartz.

I have a feeling that 'The Big Book of Metaphors' is not only going to be useful to SF therapists and their clients, but a very 'well thumbed' addition to our library. I will be recommending Kerri Formoso's book to students and practitioners alike and will be proud that it is the work of one of our enlightened colleagues.

David Newton
Hypnotherapist and Psychotherapist
DHP FAPHP MNCH MNCP SHS SQHP Sup Hyp
Director and Senior Course Lecturer
Clifton Practice Hypnotherapy Training

The Big Book of Metaphors

Introduction

Welcome to The Big Book of Metaphors, a book packed with metaphors as well as extensive, additional information that will help improve every session you carry out with clients.

As many of you pick up this book you will have no doubt experienced the same amazing, frustrating, fascinating and exhausting journey of discovery as I, to become a fully qualified hypnotherapist; trained to help people into a new way of thinking and living their lives. Some of you may still be on that journey and for those of you who are, I would say - keep going, you are on the brink of a whole new life!

I have written this book so that both new and experienced therapists have an additional guiding hand as you seek new and ever more creative ways to tailor your sessions to the incredible uniqueness of your clients.

As an experienced hypnotherapist who trained at The Clifton Practice in Bristol I have always been fully aware of the importance of using metaphors with clients. Metaphor was popularised by the 'Grandad' of hypnotherapy Milton H Erickson who recognised that helping a client see their situation in a new way had a profound effect on their ability to resolve problems. I have yet to find a book quite like this one which is entirely focused on the type of work we do and therefore every page will be relevant to you.

The Big Book of Metaphors

I have spent many years using metaphor in everyday language as most people do, to try to help others understand a new way of seeing their situation. This book is a collection of some of the most influential metaphors I have written and I am now sharing them with you so that others may benefit from them in the same way my clients have.

The metaphors in this book were written to address issues that clients have brought to me. I have found them extremely useful in helping them to see their situations in a new light, whether used while the client is in a state of hypnosis or when sharing their weekly experiences with me.

For each metaphor I have written a description of the issue I had in mind when writing it; and in some cases notes about how the client may have arrived at their situation. The book is full of information about how the mind works and processes information, solution focused therapy information and advice for adapting the metaphors to suit the client. Although I have made suggestions for the issues the metaphors were intended for, this in no way restricts their use. My decisions on which metaphor to use with clients often comes as a result of something the client brings to the session rather than the actual issue the client is struggling with. The explanation is provided only as a guide.

All of the metaphors are adaptable. One of the great joys of being a private practice hypnotherapist is being able to treat every client as a unique person, rather than trying to slot them into a 'one size fits all' treatment programme. For this reason you should always feel free to adapt any of the metaphors in any way you choose to suit an individual client, as well as your own speaking patterns and use of language – after all, it's not just our clients who are unique!

As a brain based, solution focused therapist I give my clients as much information about how the mind works as possible. With greater understanding comes greater control, and it is for this reason I have included plenty of additional information about how the mind works throughout this book.

During an initial consultation I explain the workings of the mind to the client, along with an explanation of hypnosis and how hypnotherapy will help them to overcome their problem.

For many clients, because change is being created on a subconscious level, some of the results can be subtle. For this reason I use the additional metaphor below within the initial consultation to further the client's understanding of the effect hypnosis will have.

Imagine walking into your living room and noticing that the mantelpiece needs dusting, but for one reason or another you don't get the duster and carry out the necessary job. It may be that you don't know where the duster is; you may be busy; you may think to yourself that it won't do any harm for you to leave it there for now; or it may just be that you weren't intending to do any work when you entered the room.

Each time you walk into this room you notice again that the mantelpiece needs dusting, but the job still doesn't get done. You are aware each time you enter the room that it is mildly irritating, but you don't see it as enough of a priority to do something about it.

Over time you stop noticing the dust that is gradually building. You may have been actively avoiding looking at the dust by this point, or have just got so used to it being there it doesn't register in your conscious mind any more. However, you are not as comfortable sitting in the room as you once were and you don't really know why, although you do acknowledge your discomfort each time you sit in the room.

Now, just imagine if someone were to have cleaned that mantelpiece without you knowing. It would be unlikely you would actually notice it was clear of the dust initially; after all it's not something you are giving your attention to at that point, but you do gradually become aware that you begin to feel more and more comfortable sitting in that room and the room becomes more and more pleasing to you. It may even be that it isn't until you become comfortable in the room again that you realise how uncomfortable you were previously and this helps you to appreciate and make the most of the room each and every day.

During hypnosis we are cleaning away the dust so you can be comfortable again. You can choose to check the mantelpiece regularly or you can just enjoy feeling comfortable again, but now that you understand this you can ensure that the dust never gets a chance to gather again.

In this metaphor we are explaining to the client that the presenting problem is rarely the actual problem, but a result of the gathering of dust.

The root cause of any problem a client presents with is their thought process. It is important for the client to understand that whilst the mind can usually cope with a certain amount of negative thinking - and in some circumstances these thoughts would be entirely appropriate and expected - when we continue to think and behave in these negative ways in the long term, the mind begins to view the world as a dangerous and unpleasant place to be and starts to invoke its survival mechanisms.

This is particularly evident when a client presents with anxiety/panic attacks and/or depression. Let's look at the symptoms of these conditions; increased heart rate; churning tummy; hyper-vigilance, agitation and/or a compulsion to 'hide out'. These symptoms replicate the behaviours you would expect if a sabre tooth lion were prowling around outside their house.

Unfortunately, when day to day living, coupled with habitually negative thought processes, creates these and other symptoms, it can be a little more difficult to comprehend. The metaphor above helps the client recognise the correlation between the way they think and the symptoms they are experiencing as well as how hypnotherapy helps.

The Big Book of Metaphors

In day to day life our thought processes are usually quite balanced, meaning we are able to apply logic to our circumstances and behave in a rational manner. This allows us to move through life enjoying new experiences and the company of others; feel a sense of achievement for the work we carry out; plan for the future and feel good about ourselves.

Unfortunately, there are occasions when the ratio of positive and negative thoughts become uneven and a negative thinking process can ensue. This upsets the balance of the mind and for many clients causes detrimental effects in their life. The mind becomes concentrated on everything that is, ever has been, or ever could go wrong in life. The more it focuses on this, the more negative the person becomes, triggering certain chemical responses, resulting in physiological symptoms materializing. This feeds into the negative loop. The mind is no longer functioning in a rational, logical, positive way and the thoughts continue to descend into negativity. As this happens, so the levels of stress increase and the survival part of the mind (the emotional, reactive part) assumes the worst and 'steps in' to help. This can lead to a further downward spiral as the survival mind demonstrates its characteristics of assuming the worst case scenario and focusing on problems.

It can be difficult to regain the levels of logic, rationale and positivity required to correct the balance once the survival mind has decided it is needed. For some, medication will be used to alter the chemical balance in the mind. Using medication stops the body re-absorbing the positive chemicals the brain produces so that periods of positive thinking can last for longer. However, medication does not encourage the thinking and behaviours necessary to ensure increased amounts of these chemicals are produced or reduce the activation of the survival mechanisms, so the results can be limited.

For others, hypnotherapy is the answer, either instead of or in addition to medication. Hypnotherapy works directly with the survival area of the mind to reduce the over-stimulation of the mechanisms. It also engages the area of the mind responsible for logical, rational and positive thought processes to allow solutions to be found and plans to be made without being rejected by the minds' natural preference for familiarity. Over a period of time, these more positive ways of thinking and responding become the familiar pattern that the mind prefers. This corrects the chemical balance in the long term and allows the client to proceed into their future in a more positive way.

Metaphor plays an important role in this process as it allows suggestions to be made to the subconscious in a way that is non-threatening and the "hidden" message is accepted more readily, allowing the client to view their problem in a new, sometimes previously unseen, way.

I am sure The Big Book of Metaphors will prove to be a valuable asset to hypnotherapists as well as other caring professionals and therapists. With all the additional information about the way the brain functions, how clients develop the problems they do and the suggestions for Solution Focused questioning along with all the metaphors provided, this book is a valuable tool for anyone working to help clients find solutions to problems.

Your feedback is always appreciated and can be left at www.amazon.co.uk/thebigbookofmetaphors.

I hope you continue to enjoy this wonderful journey through your career for many years to come and take pleasure every day in knowing that you have made a difference and changed the lives of each and every one of your clients.

1. Clearing Problems to Find Solutions

This metaphor is an excellent one to use near the beginning of sessions together. It addresses the issue of whether there is anything good in the client's life. There are always times where clients have been so focused on dealing with the problems they are seeking help with, they are having trouble seeing that there are 'flowers' underneath the problems.

It also addresses the fact that each client has a different experience as they move through sessions. For some clients a huge change is seen early on. These are the clients who have instinctively chosen to work on the easier parts of their problem first. On occasion they will decide that having gained sight of their 'flowers' they are then able to move forward without help and stop making appointments. As a therapist it is important to recognise they have been given the strength, tools and ability to tackle their problems by themselves and this is a good result even if they have left sessions before resolving all their problems. They will, in all likelihood, continue to resolve problems for themselves and the therapist should feel proud to have helped them on their journey.

Other clients will either choose to stay with the sessions until they have resolved the more obstinate problems or they will choose to tackle these more difficult 'weeds' first. This can sometimes be frustrating for a therapist hungry to see obvious results, as progress may appear slow, and sometimes non-existent in some sessions. Patience and belief in the process is the only way to proceed in these instances; the client **is** working on solutions, even if this is not always apparent.

This metaphor helps the client understand their options and become aware of the different ways people approach their problems and get to the solutions.

The client may even be unaware how negative they sound at the beginning of sessions and this is because of the way the mind works. Where the survival mechanisms of the mind have been repeatedly called upon, they become over sensitive and begin to create more and more problems for clients. The nature of the survival part of the mind is to think of everything in the worst case scenario and to focus attention on the difficulties. As a result of this the client will often present with more than one problem. They may not have consciously acknowledged every problem, but they are aware of the most obvious symptoms.

The metaphor ensures the client understands that therapy will be helping to clear all the problems, even if they are not consciously aware of some of them. They will however, be aware of the emergence of a 'garden' they are able to enjoy, appreciate and nurture.

Clients can sometimes get impatient to see their goals come to fruition. This metaphor reminds them that sometimes planting the seed and allowing nature to take its course, is the best way to proceed. Meanwhile they can re-direct their attention to another part of the job. This allows them to reap the benefits without becoming stressed, impatient or frustrated when obvious progress is not being made.

It can be useful to come back to this metaphor to help clients identify how they are progressing through the sessions; perhaps by asking them to notice some weeds that are now absent and naming some plants that have been sown. Helping the client to always be aware of their progress and verbalise their successes will help the client to identify what they have achieved and what more needs to be done.

From the time of Sigmund Freud and his psycho-analytical approach to problems, it has been widely believed that 'caring' professionals should be experts at guiding clients into the heart of their problems to find the origins and release any unresolved emotion connected to the problem.

This was often a very long and painful process for the client where the expectation was that they may get worse before they got better, as a result of being encouraged back into their most painful memories time and time again to re-create the emotion of the event in an effort to find resolution.

It was not unusual for a client to spend many years in therapy, sifting through every event looking for ways it may have caused their current situation. Jargon such as 'transference' and 'counter-transference' was the language used for the negative emotional responses the client sometimes (understandably in my opinion) had towards the therapist guiding them into the unpleasant memories; and for the feelings this could then stir up in the therapist.

Not only was this practice emotionally harrowing for the client, it often had an equally negative effect on the therapist. In some instances this would lead the therapist to *seek* therapy as a result of the therapy they were providing!

Many clients still expect this type of approach from therapy but thankfully, whilst it is still widely acknowledged that some 'cleaning out' of old emotions can be useful, the modern day approach generally steers very clearly towards a more humanistic and kinder way of dealing with the problems. Solution focused therapy has its basis in the belief that if a person is content and achieving in their life they are better able to process emotions and events naturally. It recognises that the quickest way to resolution for many clients is to help them towards a more positive way of thinking so they can work towards a happy, fulfilled present. This will in turn allow them to 'let go' of the past and continue through life in a more productive, emotionally stable way.

Solution focused therapy allows the client to always feel a sense of achievement for their forward movement rather than keeping them held in the problem. It also helps them to identify what has gone well and the resources they already have access to, within them. When working in this way the client is empowered to resolve their own problems, not just during sessions but well into the future.

Solution focused ways of working are growing in popularity as trainers, employers and therapists acknowledge that a positive way of working and thinking about situations is far more effective than focusing on what's going wrong. Where the client can be aware of the positives in their character and situation, they will feel far more confident to build on these. This ensures results are seen quickly and pleasantly rather than continually dragging the client back into the misery of the problem.

This metaphor helps to explain to the client that the way to a perfect garden isn't to nurture the weeds, but to clear the weeds and nurture the flowers.

The Big Book of Metaphors

A PERFECT GARDEN

And we all know the recipe for a perfect garden, don't we? Weed out the weeds and cultivate what we want…

We may look at our garden and wonder where to start. It may seem as if the weeds are everywhere, that they've taken over the whole garden and there's no hope. But when we look a bit closer we can begin to see that there definitely are flowers in our garden, although we may have to look closely and move some of those weeds to one side to find them.

Different people will decide to tackle this job in different ways. Some will decide to start with the weeds that stem from a just a few roots that have been allowed to run wild. The thing with these weeds is that they send out 'shooters' that attach themselves to the plants we want in the garden and they can seem to have killed those plants, but they haven't. The majority of these weeds, although they spread quickly, are actually quite fragile and surprisingly their roots are only just beneath the surface of the soil. This makes them really easy to pull up and gives us the impression we are clearing a lot of the problem quickly and easily and of course, this gives us a lot of pleasure and motivates us to continue the job. When we pull up these 'surface weeds' we can start to see the plants beneath; perhaps some that we'd even forgotten were there – we can begin to see the outlines of the wonderful garden that is there, it's just below the surface, waiting to show itself proudly once again...

Others will choose to go for the 'hard to shift' weeds first, that grow tall with roots that go deeper and that's a job that takes applied effort. We might need to get the garden fork to loosen those roots and we may need to put on our gardening gloves to avoid getting hurt by the spikes. It can sometimes seem that we're working really hard but not seeing much for the effort we're putting in. Of course, we know that this part of the job is just as necessary; we're clearing space, not just above the soil, but below it too and it makes a huge difference to the finished product. It's nice to know too, that if we start with these tougher weeds we then get to move onto the easier to remove ones nearer the end of the job. That means we've saved the easier bits of the problem until the end and they can be cleared quickly; almost as an afterthought.

Still others might choose to go for the logical progression around the garden. Tackling the tougher **and** the wide spread weeds alternately, each weed is removed as soon as it is identified, whether it's a surface weed or more deeply rooted.

Whichever way you choose to weed your garden we mustn't ever forget how important it is to sow new plants in the spaces. If we just clear the weeds and leave empty spaces those weeds could come back anytime.

We may not be clear at the beginning of the job how we want our garden to look – we may even say 'I just want the weeds gone, that's all', but common sense tells us, doesn't it, that we must put something in the space the weeds have left behind, after all we don't want to have to be putting this much effort into the weeding every day and every week, do we?

And although we may not know exactly how we want our finished garden to look, we do have some idea about the size and shape of it; what garden furniture we have, and we've usually got at least some vague idea of a couple of the plants that are already there, under the weeds, that we can work with, and that's an excellent start to begin building our perfect garden. We know, too that we can change our mind about the detail as we go along; we may uncover something unexpected as we weed or have to shift what's already there around a little bit, to make space for something we decide we really want – gardens are after all, flexible and never stay exactly the same…

When the time comes to plant those new seeds we can be patient – planting the seed is only the first step. We don't have to keep digging up the soil to know something is happening to that seed. We don't give up on it just because it doesn't sprout immediately; we know that the roots need to grow a little first to give it the stable base needed for it to grow strong and so we just trust that having planted the seed the plant will, in all likelihood, grow. And sometimes we have to wait a while before the fruit is edible; but we can always get on with something else while we're waiting for that to happen, can't we?

But all the time we follow the same pattern….weeding and planting; weeding then planting until our garden is so full of what we *do* want, that the pleasure we gain from it is well worth the little bit of weeding we have to do each week and the garden can support the plants so well when there are no weeds…

2. Character Types

It is not unusual during the course of working with clients to find that there are background 'mother issues'. This metaphor has been written to address this issue.

In Terence Watts' book Warriors, Settlers and Nomads he explains that we are all descendants of three main tribes of man that roamed the earth over one hundred thousand years ago. Each of these tribes had characteristics that are still in evidence in basic human nature today and account for the vast character differences that can occur between members of the same family.

He explains that a predominantly Warrior character will be an expert in planning; have little time or patience for sensitivity; are no-nonsense; like to control and are very logical and driven. Settlers will be predominantly peace-loving; nurturing; patient; care-givers who are happy to compromise and tolerate discomfort in difficult times. He describes Nomads as individuals who have a tendency to avoid deep emotional attachment; are light hearted; entertaining wanderers who like change, drama and excitement.

The book explores these three types in far more detail and explains how we would identify ourselves and others. It also explains how this information can be used to help us appreciate the wisdom and strengths that may have been laying dormant inside. The book is highly recommended and can be found at http://www.amazon.co.uk/Warriors-Settlers-Nomads-Discovering-What/dp/1899836489.

When a client presents with or reveals during sessions that they have 'mother issues' it is not unusual to identify that the client is a Settler child who has a more nurturing, accommodating nature and has been brought up by a Warrior mother who is less emotionally available and often unintentionally critical and pragmatic. The child can grow up feeling let down and angry that they have not received the nurturing they had hoped for, and this feeling can often continue into adulthood.

It is thought that because the mothers' traditional role is to love and nurture and the fathers' role to fight and protect; the break in expectation when the mother displays strong Warrior traits can lead to the child's negative and disappointed feelings. It would be true to say however, that this is not always the case and *any* deviation from what the child had expected or hoped for from their parents can lead to problems.

When a client has spent their whole life feeling criticised or rejected by the person they expected to receive warm, comforting, nurturing behaviours from, the client's core belief system about themselves can become altered. As children (if they are attending as an adult) they may have suffered, and continue to suffer, from a lack of confidence, feelings of not being good enough and an inability to take charge of their own life. As adults they may feel resentment towards the parent and harbour lots of thoughts of how things could have been had they experienced the type of parent they perceive others have.

These thoughts and feelings can have a detrimental effect upon the client. This metaphor encourages calmness and acceptance of the situation, with a subtle indication that although they may not have had the parent they hoped for, they are certainly able to find love and nurturing from other sources.

Remember, this metaphor can be adapted to suit other situations the client is struggling with, simply by changing the type of book 'Rebecca' was hoping to get. It could, for instance, be used for someone who has an illness they will have to live with simply by changing the 'hoped for' novel to one about a being fit and healthy. As long as the content of the novel in the story has some slight similarity (and it is suggested it is only a slight similarity) rather than paraphrasing the client's specific difficulty, then the subconscious will pick up on the message of acceptance.

It is also worth mentioning here that the author's main client base is female and therefore most of the metaphors centre on female characters. For male clients, all metaphors can be adapted by using male names to ensure that they are able to identify more readily with the story.

The Big Book of Metaphors

ACCEPTING WHAT YOU GET

….and as I talk to you here as you lie so comfortably there… I'm reminded of my friend Rebecca one Christmas…..her heart's desire on this particular Christmas was a book….it was a romantic novel that she'd seen the cover of in shops and knew that some of her friends had….and she was looking forward so much to having this book….she knew that she'd be able to snuggle up in bed, all warm and cosy, with this book and it would bring her so much pleasure and hold her attention so well….she knew enough about the story that she already knew this book had almost been written for her….it was like the author had listened to her deepest thoughts and needs and written the story just to suit her….and so Rebecca was looking forward to this Christmas morning when she'd get exactly what she wanted under the tree…..

With excitement she rose early on Christmas morning and hurried down the stairs….there under the tree was the present….it could only be the book she'd wanted, the shape and size of the present was exactly right, she recognised a book when she saw one, even when it was wrapped up in shiny paper with a big bow on the top….and she couldn't wait to begin enjoying that book….

When it came to present opening time, Rebecca could actually see the book in her minds' eye, could see herself reading it, feeling so warm and comforted by it, and as the present was passed to her she couldn't wait to rip off the wrapper, this was what she'd wanted…..

Imagine her disappointment when she finally got into that present and found, not a romantic novel but an encyclopaedia! She was crushed, she was furious, she felt cheated; this was not what she'd asked for, not at all! She tossed the book away angrily, feeling so let down. Who wanted a crummy encyclopaedia? Not her that was for sure! It wasn't going to make good bedtime reading. It wasn't going to carry her away to a world of happiness and love; it was useless to her, pointless, a waste of a present, why would anyone think she'd want an encyclopaedia? She might as well throw it away for all the good it was going to do her….

….and then, something happened, just as she was about to pick the book up and throw it in the rubbish bin to show what she thought of what she'd got, she noticed the page was open and a word seemed to almost jump off the page at her. 'Anger – an emotion resulting from refusal to accept things as they are. Love is considered to be the opposite of anger, is said to be unconditional acceptance'. Her attention was caught. She looked further up the page to see what was said about Acceptance – a person's assent to the reality of a situation, recognising without attempting to change, protest or exit. As her eyes moved over the pages, she began to learn more and more about what she had been given and found that, although it may not be what she'd hoped for, it didn't make it worthless; there was value in this gift she'd been given; a value that she'd not been able to see at first; she could learn from this gift, she could become wiser, a better person, this book was one she could benefit from for the rest of her life, one that could sit on her bookshelf and be accessed when she needed answers that couldn't be found anywhere else. And as she began to think about all the uses this encyclopaedia could have for her she felt her good humour returning, she smiled and continued opening presents from under the tree, happy and willing to accept what she got with an open mind….

And do you know that she realised too, she hadn't needed to have a copy of that romantic novel herself, when she wanted to snuggle down and read that particular story she was able to read someone else's copy and the story was just as good – especially with the additional knowledge of the words she'd gained from the encyclopaedia that was always around somewhere should she need it….

The Big Book of Metaphors

3. Procrastination

This is an excellent metaphor that helps the client understand what they need to do to make the journey into their preferred future.

It addresses the fact that sometimes the solution can take time, effort, and the occasional diversion, but makes it very clear that having a vivid idea of where they want to be will allow them to always travel in the right direction.

It also makes an extremely important point to clients that they need to put action behind their wishes. It is not enough to just talk the talk in sessions; taking action is the key to making changes.

Procrastination can often be in evidence with clients. This simply means that the survival mechanism has been over-activated and the client has become 'immobilised'. To understand how this activation of the survival mechanism can affect a client's behaviours, it is often simplest to turn to the animal world for answers.

Animals do not share the large intellectual area of the brain that humans have developed and so the majority of their 'survival' behaviours are much easier to observe. For example, if you watch a cat who has suddenly been startled, they will often run away (avoidance) or stay to fight (anger). Where they sense there is danger but are not sure where that danger is, or if they are unsure of the power of their aggressor, they will become prone (procrastination) in the hope of gaining sufficient information to know how to proceed. In these cases the cat not only has insufficient intellect to rely upon, but also has experienced a sharp rise in anxiety, so the effects are very obvious. As humans, the intellect usually maintains some control which subdues these instincts and because the anxiety being experienced is of the chronic type that has increased gradually over time rather than a sharp, instant rise, the responses can be more subtle but are still evident.

The chemical response to stress in the mind contributes hugely to the lack of motivation many clients can display. Where this "freeze" instinct has been triggered the mind reduces the production of motivating chemicals leading to feelings of lethargy and despondency. As the client begins once again to become physically and socially active and have a more positive approach, the production of serotonin, endorphins and noradrenalin increases. As this happens the client begins to feel more motivated, which in turn leads to even more production of these chemicals in the brain.

In a client who is displaying many depressive symptoms it may be unlikely that they would be able to take any major steps in this direction early in the sessions. That said it is important to never underestimate a client's internal resources or motivation. It is also important never to set up a negative expectation of what the client will be capable of achieving between sessions. For many though, progress is likely to be slower and something as small as leaving the house to take a short walk can be the 'breakthrough' that allows them to reap the benefits that will give them the motivation to do more and eventually 'climb aboard the bus'.

Goal setting and planning can allow the client to see they do have sufficient information to proceed and this will help them to leave their procrastination behind and see the future in a way that appeals to them.

In solution focused therapy the emphasis is always on times when the client has felt better, even if only slightly, and the problem has been reduced or absent. When clients begin to talk about their achievements or dreams for the future the mind instantly responds with heightened, positive chemical responses. The client moves into a more positive frame of mind and the left pre-frontal cortex of the brain engages. This area of the brain is responsible for decision making, planning and problem solving. When a client has engaged this area of the brain immediately prior to experiencing hypnosis, maximum benefit will be seen from their time on the couch and they will begin to become aware of the process this metaphor describes happening in their own life.

The Big Book of Metaphors

BUS STOPS

If you're standing at a bus stop does that mean you're going to get to your destination?

Well, the first thing you'd need to know is where you want to get to. I think you'd agree it would be difficult to get there if you don't know where you want to get to. Of course, you could just get on a bus and leave it to chance, hope for the best – but you could end up somewhere you don't want to be, you might even get lost along the way.

So once you know where you want to get to, the next step is to check which bus you need to catch to get there – it might take a little research and thought to plan your journey – you might find you have to take more than one bus, and you know how the bus service is – there may not be a direct route to where you want to go, and sometimes you may have to go a little out of your way, but that's ok, as long as you know your destination you'll know whether you're still on track to get there, no matter which route you have to take.

You'll need to know which buses to get on and where to make the changes; you'll need to have an idea of the timing too...

So once you know all this – does *this* mean you'll get to your destination? Well, only if you actually *get* **on the bus** and **stay on the bus** and **make the changes** you need to along the way – and of course, you'll have to keep observing the scenery carefully to make sure you recognise how *you are getting closer* to your destination and when **you are** arriving *at the place you want to be...*

4. Weight Loss

Hypnotherapy is being increasingly sought nowadays to help with weight loss. There are many techniques using hypnosis to help the client overcome their problem and different techniques will have different success rates depending on the client.

This metaphor addresses some of the beliefs that clients have around food in acknowledgement of the fact that these often contribute towards the overall struggle they have with their eating habits. An example is the ingrained rule, often brought from childhood, that they must finish every bit of food on the plate. For some clients this will not have been a problem when a parent was in charge of portion control, but has become a problem as the size of their portions has increased, and occasionally, the size of the plate too!

It also tackles the modern problem of "all you can eat" and 'bargains' such as supermarket offers. Where beliefs about money and food become intertwined they often (if you'll pardon the pun) feed off each other.

This metaphor also reminds the client of the effects they are probably already feeling carrying the additional weight and the potential health problems they could be heading for if they continue to 'fill up' in the way they have been.

Where someone has been brought up being told they must eat everything on their plate, that wasted food is wasted money, that it is rude to leave food, or one of the many other phrases frequently used with children where food is concerned, these beliefs will have been laid down in the long term memory and have become subconscious beliefs. In many cases the phrases were coupled with some sort of emotional signal; such as the threat of punishment or guilt. When emotion is attached to a thought or instruction the subconscious belief is generated much more quickly. For some children, the indication was given that food is the most suitable reward for good behaviour or results; could replace affection; or take pain away. These beliefs were created in such instances as a cream cake being given as a way of congratulating them on an achievement; sweets given to a crying child to make them feel better or food treats being given in place of a cuddle or other show of love. These too will have formed neural connections that are now residing in the client's subconscious, leading to a belief system which integrates food with love and eating appears to be the path to creating happy, positive feelings.

The human brain contains approximately 100 billion neurons. Each time we hear an instruction, have a thought or carry out a behaviour, the neurons involved fire an electrical impulse to each other. The more often this is repeated the easier it is for the neurons to make the connection. Once these electrical impulses reach 'critical mass' they start producing proteins that lay the thought, instruction or behaviour down in the long term memory so that conscious thought is not required to carry them out and they become subconscious beliefs that make up the core belief system.

It is for this reason that the client often finds it difficult to maintain the necessary eating habits for weight loss. Each time the client attempts a sustained change in the way they eat, they are working against the core beliefs that have been planted and re-enforced throughout their lives. The more they attempt to fight against these beliefs, the higher the anxiety levels become, and subsequently the more difficult it becomes to maintain the intellectual control necessary to ensure sensible eating. It is often necessary through sessions to help the client be aware of this core belief system, so that they can begin to develop new, more helpful beliefs that will lead to a more healthy eating habit and subsequently the weight loss they are seeking.

As each client will have been brought up with differing beliefs in place where food is concerned it is difficult to write a metaphor that matches all of them. However, through experience, the issues addressed in this metaphor are some of the more common ones clients struggle with and therefore will be useful for a great many weight loss clients.

As well as addressing these core beliefs it is also important to work to lower the client's overall stress levels. With reduced stress levels the client is able to retain increased intellectual control. When the intellect is in charge the client stays motivated and makes the right choices about food in the long term.

Reduced stress also leads to reduced cortisol production in the brain. Cortisol is a stress hormone that 'clings on' to fat. This response is part of the survival mechanism of the mind. The production of cortisol to retain fat is a defence mechanism against the possibility of food being unavailable. When the mind becomes aware of increased stress it believes there is potentially life threatening danger around and so will want to hang on to all the energy resources the body has to fuel 'fight or flight' should it be required.

In modern Western society it is very unusual to have a deficit of food so the client continues to eat as much or more than they need, while the brain continues to release cortisol to keep a hold of the fat content of that food.

For many clients, the idea of 'going on a diet' itself causes increased anxiety as they imagine the deprivation and social implications of not being able to indulge in 'normal' eating habits. Hypnotherapy seeks to encourage the client into healthy eating, with the emphasis on moderation and filling the time in between meals more constructively rather than 'dieting' which helps to alleviate this initial rise in anxiety. Understanding the role of cortisol in previous weight loss attempts also eases the possibility of frustration the client may have previously felt having suffered deprivation and seen few results.

This knowledge of how the mind/body system works along with the reduction of overall stress achieved by hypnotherapy, will allow the mind to 'let go' of the fat reserves and the client begins to lose weight naturally.

Sleep is also an area that needs to be addressed in clients who are seeking to lose weight. Most weight loss clients will have been experiencing some kind of sleep disturbance. Studies have found that clients who regularly sleep less than 5 hours per night have a 15% increase of ghrelin, the hormone that instigates feelings of hunger, and 15% less leptin, the hormone that suppresses the appetite. This lack of sleep or disturbance in sleep will also increase a client's stress levels and inhibit their ability to retain the intellectual control necessary to 'side-step' their core beliefs.

Relaxation CDs, such as those given out by many hypnotherapists, serve an important role in improving sleep patterns. The client should be encouraged to listen to these CDs each night as they go to sleep. As the mind learns to switch off and relax when the client gets into bed, a more productive sleep habit will quickly take hold.

The Big Book of Metaphors

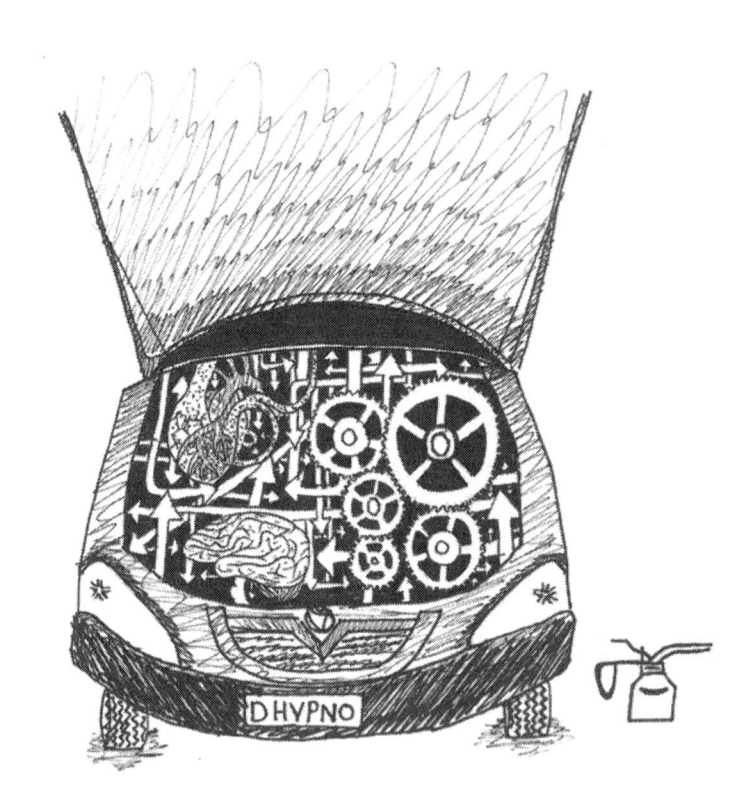

CLAPPED OUT CAR

What would you do if you had a car that you regularly filled with oil and it ran and ran, for miles and miles and worked in perfect order – but then as time wore on you noticed that the more often you filled up with oil, the more it seemed to need? Would you reduce the amount of oil you put in each time, or would you keep filling it up – just because you once believed this to be a good thing?

What about if the car started to become sluggish and the steering heavier and heavier the more you filled it up? Would you put less in it then – or keep filling it up because the oil was on offer so using more seemed to be offering value for money?

How about if the wheels got stiff or the axle kept groaning – would you keep filling up, perhaps mixing it with a lot of cheap stuff because you knew other people who continually 'fill up' and often use inferior products and you wanted to fit in with them?

Would you wait for the engine to seize, or for it to slow down so much that you had difficulty getting it out of the garage?

Or will you do the smart thing – reduce how much you're putting in; use only the quality stuff; watch it return to its former glory and enjoy the money you ultimately save?

I wonder what you'll choose to do...

5. Mirror Neurons

It's not unusual for clients to be dissatisfied or unhappy in their workplace and this can have a detrimental effect on other areas of their life. Often they do not feel in a position to leave their place of work so this metaphor was written as a way of helping them cope better with their work environment. It encourages them to display a happy demeanour in work to help activate a more positive attitude, improve their colleagues' moods and help them appreciate the good things about their workplace.

A cluster of the 100 billion neurons in the brain are 'mirror neurons'. These neurons identify and replicate facial expressions and body language. They are constantly active and can have a positive or negative effect on our mood depending on who we are encountering in our day to day living.

The mirror neurons make a huge contribution to our ability to interact with the world; they are our connection to others. When someone smiles at another person the mirror neurons unconsciously pick up that smile. The mirror neurons automatically activate the muscle system and soon the smile appears on the face of the other person, along with a positive chemical response in the brain. A smile is a very obvious example as few people can resist smiling back at someone who is smiling at them, and they are often fully aware of this response.

These mirror neurons work in the same way with any signal they are given each and every moment of each and every day. When the client walks along a busy street for instance, their mirror neurons are constantly identifying the facial expressions and body language of every person they pass, activating the muscle system to a greater or lesser degree and instigating a chemical response to match that muscle movement. If they are paying little attention to those they pass in the street, or the people they pass are not known to them, the response is minimal, but still there. Where they are more attentive to another's expressions, the moods the mirror neurons detect literally become contagious. Studies have shown the more emotionally connected people are the more susceptible they are to each others' signals. Each time these mirror neurons are activated they respond by instigating full or micro muscle movements, so the recipient may or may not be aware of their response, but the chemical response in the body will become altered as a result of the information picked up by the neurons.

Where the behaviours, thoughts and attitudes being displayed are positive the benefits are obvious. Unfortunately though, the mirror neurons also carry out the same muscle and chemical response to negative facial expressions and body language. The effect of this is that it is possible to become very stressed, depressed or dissatisfied purely by being around others that feel this way.

In the workplace, especially during this economic downturn, interactions with unhappy members of staff can lead to a mass dissatisfaction amongst the workforce through the contagion that occurs because of the mirror neurons, rendering the workplace an extremely unhappy place to be.

With this knowledge of the mirror neurons, clients can begin to understand some of the reasons their workplace may have become such an unhappy place and can feel empowered to do something about this. When a client is in possession of this knowledge of the mirror neurons they can very quickly and easily test and demonstrate their power simply by leaving the session and smiling at other people on their way out. Not only will the client be spreading happiness and proving what they have just learned, but they will also be receiving, through their own mirror neurons, an added positive chemical response when those they have smiled at return the smile.

Happiness quite literally, is contagious and it is always beneficial when this is remembered. It can be hugely encouraging for the client to imagine what sort of world it would be if everyone chose to take the position of Director of Happiness and how easy it would be to spread that happiness.

David Hamilton PhD is an expert in the area of mirror neurons and his book 'The Contagious Power of Happiness' is highly recommended, as are the talks he regularly schedules in the UK and around the world. More details can be found at www.drdavidhamilton.com.

With this knowledge of the mirror neuron system clients often evaluate their interactions with others. They begin to see the impact others are having on them and also the impact they may be having on others. By becoming consciously aware in this way the client can choose to adapt their behaviours to have a more positive impact on those around them and in turn experience a more positive response from others.

This information regarding the mirror neuron system is also particularly helpful for clients struggling with social interactions generally; perhaps clients who are starting a new job, college or school. With this understanding they can begin to see how a nervous demeanour, where eye contact is avoided and smiles are rare, is picked up by the mirror neuron system of others and reflected back. Where the client makes a conscious effort to make eye contact with others and smile, a friendly response is far more likely. Clients can have the confidence to do this knowing that even if the recipient doesn't show the reflected smile, they are in fact smiling on the inside, without being consciously aware of it. It can be comforting to know they have passed the happiness to another person who might continue to infect others in this positive way.

The Big Book of Metaphors

The Big Book of Metaphors

DIRECTOR OF HAPPINESS

And now I'm going to tell you about a very special new job that you've been given…..it's a job that no-one else knows about, a job that is especially for you to carry out during your day to day living, at the office, at home, in your social life….your new job title is Director of Happiness…..that's right the **Director** of **Happiness**…..and this is a very special job for you to carry out…..your job now is to spread as much happiness as you can to as many people as you can…..and this is a job given to you because **you are a very happy person**

…..you spread joy to all those who come into contact with you…..you share a smile with all those who see you and in this way you share happiness…..and did you know that when you give a little piece of happiness the person you give it to has no choice but to accept it…..that's right, when you give happiness away it is always accepted……your job is to give happiness…..because **you are a very positive person**…..and you can be positive in every situation…..and it's a very important job to be the Director of Happiness……

Other people feel happy in your company as you share your smile, your sense of humour, your positive outlook on life and in this way you spread the happiness, not only to those who come into contact with you directly, but also to those who come into contact with those you have infected with happiness......this is how your new job works, you give happiness to those you come into contact with and they in turn, give that happiness to the people they come into contact with......so you can see how very important this job is, and how important it is for you to do this job well......

And I wonder how many people you can infect tomorrow with happiness? And the next day.....and the next.....and I wonder how many people will benefit from this giving of happiness? I wonder how long it will take you to infect everyone at work with happiness when it starts spreading, and the more it spreads the quicker it spreads.....and you have that very important job because **you are a very happy and positive person.**

And this very important job of Director of Happiness has the best salary attached to it that you could ask for......you feel so lucky to have been picked for this job......each time you give someone some happiness you receive happiness back, and the happiness you receive back is even more valuable than the happiness you gave away, because you know that you earned that happiness and you improved someone else's day when you gave away that piece of happiness……..so you can see how you could easily become rich on happiness when you start to give it away…..just knowing that you made a difference to someone else's day……

And I wonder how many times someone's given you a little piece of happiness and they didn't even know they had…..and how powerful that happiness has been…..and now you're in charge of giving that happiness out……

Who will be the first person to receive that happiness do you think? Will you start with the happiest person you know and give them some more happiness, or will you start with the most unhappy person you know? But it really doesn't matter, because happiness is so easy to give and receive……when someone is happy to you, you always accept that happiness, and when you give happiness to others they have no choice but to accept a little piece of that happiness…..and this very important job that's been given to someone who is **very happy and positive** starts right now, today, this moment….. and I wonder how many people can you infect with this happiness?

The Big Book of Metaphors

6. Brain Wave Activity

With over 900,000,000 people worldwide estimated to be using Facebook this metaphor is one that many clients understand and identify with, although care must be taken to ensure it is relevant for your client. If a client has never had Facebook or a computer or is avidly against using Facebook as a social media then it wouldn't be appropriate to use this metaphor.

For many people, however, they will be able to identify closely with this metaphor and the concept of deleting unwanted items from timeline; deciding who they want to interact with and the idea of setting goals within the context of the work that needs to be done in a way they can understand clearly.

For teenagers and young adults this metaphor could have the added advantage of helping build rapport. When these young clients hear a therapist (someone they often regard as an authority figure with which they have no connection) talking 'their' language it often has the effect of helping them open up in a way that feels safe and familiar to them.

It also taps into the unconscious desire experienced by many Facebook users to be seen as popular by way of receiving lots of 'likes' by people viewing their profile in acknowledgement of them having said or done something that their Facebook friends and family approve of. It is important to never under-estimate the value of this 'mass approval' and to recognise that the vast majority of users; both young and old, do enjoy this public display of popularity and will often 'play' to their audience.

By the time clients approach a hypnotherapist they often feel out of control in many areas of their life and are confused by where to start to begin sorting out the problems. By putting it into the context of Facebook, clients are able to see a structure and can decide which part to work on first. They identify with the feeling of control that comes from having their life 'laid out' as a profile and that they have control over the decisions about what to keep, what to delete and what to edit.

A Facebook timeline replicates a diary of sorts and the client may be able to identify the contributing factors to periods when they were happy or not, through previous statuses. It may also serve to help them identify where their thought patterns have become very negative – for anyone who's ever used Facebook, there are usually at least one or two friends on someone's friends list who seem to post statuses that are always negative, displaying to the world, even if they are unaware of it themselves, their negative state of mind. This metaphor may help raise the clients awareness and they may realise they have become one of those people. They may decide to begin changing their status updates to more positive ones, leading them to making an active effort to look out for the positives in their life to use as subjects.

The text is deliberately confusional so that the client's focus of attention stays on the message rather than wandering in the direction of what is actually happening on their Facebook account. It is recommended that the penultimate paragraph is said at a speed just a little quicker than usual and that a pause of approximately 30-60 seconds is left at the end. In this pause the client will be picturing status updates, photographs, friend's lists and the possibility of gaining outside approval for their actions.

Whilst the client will feel extremely relaxed on the couch, sometimes so relaxed they may snore, and the hypnotherapist can see that they are visibly relaxed, their minds are incredibly busy during this time particularly during an active metaphor such as this one. Modern technology such as functional magnetic resonance imaging (fMRI), positron emission tomography (PET) and single-photon emission computed tomography (SPECT) is able to show scientists exactly what is happening during this time. With the help of these types of technology they have been able to uncover the details of the brainwave activity that occurs while the client is relaxing and visualising.

When clients are asked to close their eyes at the beginning of the hypnosis process their brain wave activity changes. They move from Beta brainwave activity (associated with being alert) to Alpha brainwaves. This opens up communication between areas of the brain and allows the client to become relaxed in both body and mind. Alpha brainwaves are associated with clear thinking, problem solving, positive thinking and increased creativity. When the brain is creating Alpha brainwaves the production of serotonin is increased.

As the client is guided into hypnosis the brainwave activity slows further to Theta brainwaves. These induce a state of deep relaxation where the client connects fully with their subconscious, allowing heightened intuition and peak levels of creativity. This deeply relaxed state allows the client to 'hyper focus' – remain intensely focused and motivated - and is also associated with boosted learning abilities.

In this Theta brainwave state the client is able to begin to picture more positive actions. They also engage the anterior cingulate of the brain whose job it is to come up with solutions based on the request made in the form of the pictures created. Interference from the Conscious Critical Factor is also reduced. This area of the brain is the 'gateway' between the conscious and subconscious and decides whether something fits in with current beliefs or behaviours. Its usual function when active is to reject suggestions that do not fit in with the client's current beliefs or ways of thinking. With interference from the Conscious Critical Factor reduced, the client is able to come up with new and creative solutions to old problems. It is important to allow the mind the time to do this while the client is in trance and a lengthy pause allows this time for the answers to become more evident to the client. When this happens the client is far more likely to take decisive action following the session.

By being able to anticipate a positive status update the client is adding positive emotion to positive thought and this increases motivation. The client will find it easy to hold the idea of a status update in mind and therefore take the necessary action to ensure that this update appears on their timeline at some point.

The added bonus to this metaphor is that the client will be reminded of the work being done each time they engage with Facebook, and for many clients this will be daily, and will therefore not only be looking for signs every day of improvement but also will be reminded each time to adopt positive thought and action in their life.

The Big Book of Metaphors

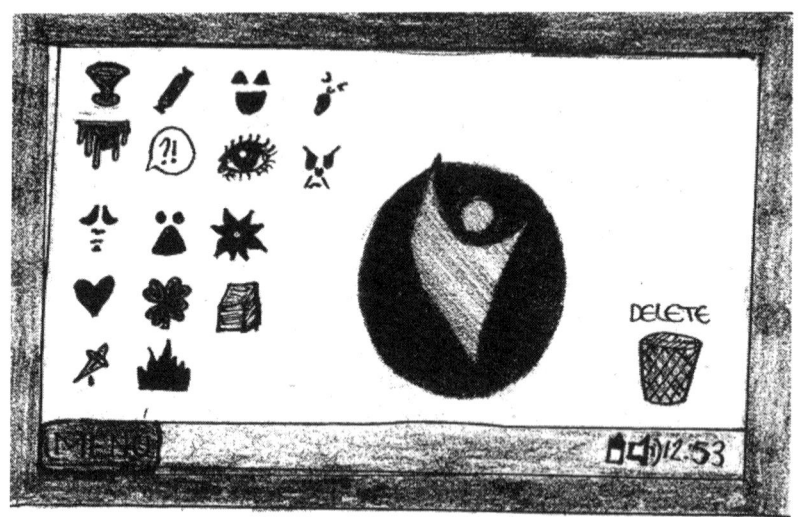

FACEBOOK TIMELINE

And have you ever wished life was a little bit more like a Facebook timeline? When you can delete a status or a comment or a picture because it doesn't 'fit' with how you want to be seen, how you want to remember, how you want to feel…

And isn't it great how you hit that delete button and it disappears from your timeline as though it never existed – and once it's deleted it's gone and forgotten so quickly, so easily – that only the statuses and comments and pictures that make you happy get to stay there – and the happier you are the more fun it all is, the more likes you get, and the more people you talk to the more friends you make –

And the settings allow you to limit the comments you hear and choose to only listen to those who make you feel good – and the pictures show all the best of you and your life, and those you don't like can easily be deleted, so quickly, no fuss, no agonising, just taken out and gone forever, choosing history as you go along – deleting the history if it's not good for you and you're always in control of everything you choose is relevant – or irrelevant – and free to make the choice of how you appear and what you see when you look through your own historic timeline.

And have you ever chosen your status update the day before? Deciding what you want the world to see you've been having so much fun tomorrow and the next day and the next…and how you can choose what statuses you'll be looking back on next week, next month, next year that make you smile and fill with pride – that bring excitement and a memory of your history being created as your status updates with all the declarations of what you once thought were hopes and dreams <u>now</u> becoming realities as the albums are built and the pictures fill with colour and your 'info' changes your status or your work or your 'interested in'; the future becoming the present; the past something you can choose to keep or to delete that which serves no purpose for you and never did –

The 'Likes' increasing, congratulating, so pleasing, the LOL's the OMG's – the You Tube link to your highest potential and achievement – the views increasing, the smiley faces – the hearts and kisses – and life is like a Facebook timeline; you choose, you create, you display, you receive – and it is all under your control how you choose to see or not to hear and how you choose to keep or delete what helps and what's not…

And which status will you choose <u>now</u> to post tomorrow or next week?...

The Big Book of Metaphors

7. Insomnia

This is a great metaphor to use with clients who are struggling with insomnia or those who find it difficult to 'switch off'. They are usually identifiable by the way they speak at a very fast pace and it is sometimes difficult to get a word in before they're interrupting with a response.

These clients are often aware they need to take 'time out' and will sometimes go so far as to actually sit down for a short period of time each day with this intention. Unfortunately, although the body is less mobile, the mind is still running at a hundred miles per hour.

A good sleep pattern is essential to the well-being of clients. When carrying out an initial consultation it is always a good idea to ask about the client's sleep pattern as this will be an extremely good indicator of their general well-being.

The vast majority of clients will admit to some type of sleep disturbance and for some this will have developed into the presenting problem of insomnia.

It is generally understood that the role of slow wave sleep is important to regeneration of the body and that sleep deprivation is a known method of torture, but few understand the role of Rapid Eye Movement (REM); the dream state. Many books have been written about dream interpretation and much thought can often be given to the meaning of particular dreams but there is usually little attention paid to the purpose of dreaming.

Throughout the day, thoughts, actions and experiences generate emotion. It would not be viable for all these emotions to be expressed or experienced fully at the time they are created so the brain has to 'store' them. During REM sleep whatever generated the emotion is replayed, either literally or metaphorically, through dreams and the emotion is processed and moved from 'storage' into the intellect so that it can be released. The brain is 'cleansed' of pent up emotion and the person awakens able to move through the day in a calm and rational way.

Where a client is 'storing' too much emotion, either through a traumatic event that has produced too much emotion to process easily, or through repeated negative thinking, actions and interactions, the brain struggles to process everything being stored. This processing uses up a great deal of energy and for this reason the amount of processing the brain carries out is limited. Where there is too much being stored, the brain will wake up the dreamer to stop an excess of energy being utilised in this way.

Unfortunately, this interruption of sleep results in a build-up of residual emotion being stored. This leads the client to more negative thoughts, actions and interactions and the cycle of interrupted sleep and stored residual negative emotions continues to create excessive anxiety, stress and depression.

As the client sinks into this cycle the survival mechanisms recognise that the anxiety has increased, have no idea why and begin to respond with hyper-vigilant responses; an increased alertness, increased adrenalin secretion, psycho motor agitation and other associated symptoms. This in turn makes it very difficult for the client to experience any real relaxation and therefore overcome their symptoms.

It is important to take into consideration the client's age when using this metaphor as those below a certain age may not have experience or clear memory of what the TV screen looked like when a video was paused. DVDs do not produce the same effect as they pause with complete clarity and quality retained and therefore do not produce the same understanding within the subconscious that the metaphor is designed to ignite.

Speaking with a slow pace indicated with ellipsis will help the client's mind slow down as you use this metaphor. It is important to be aware that clients presenting with this difficulty can find it as much of a struggle to relax on the couch as they do in day to day life. It is recommended that an action induction, confusional induction or one designed to overload the mind is used for these clients. This works with their natural compulsion towards a busy mind rather than trying to encourage them to relax and switch off as their worry at their inability to do this can result in a longer induction time becoming necessary.

A client with high anxiety and/or insomnia will initially feel a compulsion to try to 'keep up' with what is being said while on the couch. By using the suggested induction techniques the therapist is 'playing' to the client's natural compulsion. However, when the mind becomes 'overloaded' with information or too confused by it, the conscious part of the brain gives up in its effort to keep up and allows the subconscious to take over. By using these techniques, induction is achieved easily without pressure being put on the client to relax. Lots of variation in speed, tone and volume of voice will also help as will moving around the room, if possible.

Once this state has been achieved the session would continue at the usual pace and volume and the metaphor can be a useful way of deepening the trance in the latter part of the session, as well as helping the client to understand the concept of true relaxation.

The Big Book of Metaphors

The Big Book of Metaphors

FAST FORWARD

I wonder if you can remember when we used to use video recorders? How wonderful it was to discover that you never needed to miss a TV programme...changing our thinking and our routines...instead of being irritated that we were going to miss something, we could relax, knowing that we had all the time in the world, that the programme would be there when we were ready for it...so wonderful to be able to rent a film and relax and enjoy that film when the time was right for us...able to watch any film we chose...pick a film to match our mood...or perhaps to *produce* the mood we wanted...a comedy to make us laugh, a weepy to make us cry, a drama to inspire us, or a fast paced action film to energise us...or something soothing and easy to watch... to... slow... us... down... becoming... more... and... more... relaxed... and... perhaps... so... relaxed... that... your... eyes... just... closed... for...a...moment...in... time...and that's fine...because you can be relaxed in the knowledge that there will always be another time to watch your film...a better time...or maybe right now...

And do you remember what you did when you wanted to do something else? Or when you just needed to rest from the film for a while? When you needed a 'time out'? Perhaps you press the 'pause' button...and the film stays still for a moment or longer...but that 'pause' button can create problems of its own...

The film flickers, the picture becomes agitated...it wants to keep on going...it wants to move forward...it's stretching and straining...not really still, just restrained...almost as if it's against its will...desperate to get going again...and of course, all this straining to get going again causes the tape to become stretched, strained, damaged...the picture distorts, the colour drains, the sounds become wobbly, the film is no longer quite so enjoyable or easy to watch...in fact, it's become quite an effort to watch it.

So what's the answer? The answer is that sometimes a pause is not quite good ...enough....we actually have to stop...just like you're doing right now. A pause stretches, strains and *re*strains...but to press the 'stop' button is to turn off totally and completely...for a moment...or longer. To stop the film, the tape, the mechanisms...so the dialogue is silenced and the tape goes slack and the picture can just disappear while you relax so wonderfully there on the couch – truly recharging – the stop button pressed for a moment in time – preserving the tape, the film as you relax THERE now and I talk to you HERE and you can know that by pressing the 'stop' button every once in a while that film will run much better and last so much longer, and stay in such good condition...while still bringing all the pleasure any film should bring...

The Big Book of Metaphors

8. Solution Focused Therapy

A solution focused approach to life and to therapy is still an alien concept to many. It was believed for many years that the answer to a problem lay in the problem. For this reason many still continue to sink themselves deeper and deeper into problem thinking, in the hope of finding the solution. There is a wonderful analogy that describes why solution focused therapy is so effective; If you are walking in the snow and your problem is that you are cold, do you sit down in the snow, inspect every snow flake and roll around in it to get warm? Or do you move away from the snow, find a warm house and light a fire?

When the focus of attention is on the problem the mind is re-creating it over and over again. Memories are not stored in the mind like DVDs, where the original film is re-run over and over again. Only the title of the film is stored. Each time a request is made for the film the brain re-creates the whole experience. This re-creation will never be an exact replica of the original because, through the very experience of life, the brain being used to re-create the experience changes, and therefore can never be exactly the same brain that experienced the event originally. Where a negative event is being re-created the mind will respond to the 'memory' by releasing some of the same negative emotional and chemical responses that event originally produced, because the mind cannot tell the difference between imagination and reality. This is evidenced very clearly when one thinks about their favourite food, or eating salt and vinegar crisps or even sucking on a lemon. The corresponding physical effect of these thoughts is a watering mouth. The brain has not been able to differentiate between the reality of eating these mouth-watering foods and the imagining of them. By consistently re-creating problem events, negative emotion, physiology and negative chemical responses are being encouraged. The result of this can be the client sinking further and further into the symptomology that has led them to seek help in the first place.

Solution focused therapy is gaining in popularity as it becomes understood that regaining a positive frame of mind and moving towards solutions benefits clients far more. When the client is in a positive frame of mind they are able to process the emotion of the negative event and are able to view it from a logical and rational viewpoint. An extension of the analogy explains this well: When someone is sitting in front of the warm fire feeling the warmth, they know the snow outside is cold, but it is no longer a problem to them. It's also much easier for them to plan how to deal with the snow from the warmth of the armchair.

Solution focused questioning and answering is a simple concept, but this doesn't necessarily make it easy. Many clients struggle with solution focused questions and spend much of their time talking about what they don't want. This type of answer comes from focusing on the problem rather than the solution. The brain cannot differentiate between what we do want and what we don't want, it only focuses on the object in question. For instance, if the instruction 'do NOT think about a blue cat' is given, it's a reasonable bet that blue cats will be an immediate thought, and will be pictured in the brain. This can have an adverse effect for the client where the mind seeks to present to them the very thing they are saying they don't want. The client's thought process is often 'I don't want to be so tired'; 'I don't want all this stress'; 'I don't want to be thinking/acting this way' etc., rather than 'I want to feel energised'; 'I want to be calm and relaxed'; 'I want a clear, focused thought process'. Solution focused questioning ensures that the client is always focused on what they **do** want; the solution.

Insoo Kim Berg and Steve de Shazer founded the Brief Family Therapy Centre in Milwaukee and were pioneers of Solution Focused Brief Therapy. They achieved outstanding results with clients using this technique, often working with clients who had been referred to them through the courts or social services and could therefore lack motivation at the outset. Their clients often had limited income and/or education and on occasions lacked the social or life skills some would think were necessary to resolve problems.

Of the many books they wrote on the subject, 'Interviewing for Solutions' by Insoo Kim Berg in collaboration with Peter de Jong is highly recommended as an introduction to working with clients in a solution focused way. This book has many practical examples of using this style of questioning with clients. More information can be found at http://www.amazon.com/Interviewing-Solutions-Introduction-Psychotherapy-Practice.

All training provided by The Clifton Practice Hypnotherapy Training College is solution focused, as their innovative approach to training always mirrors the very latest in successful techniques and modern research. They also, on occasion, offer courses in Solution Focused

Brief Therapy as an advanced course for practicing hypnotherapists. Information can be found at www.cpht.co.uk.

In recognition of the success of solution focused working practices when applied in hypnotherapy The Association for Solution Focused Hypnotherapists was established in 2010. The Association not only supports and informs hypnotherapists who work in a solution focused way; it also seeks to educate the general public and provide a register of solution focused therapists for them. This allows the general public to find hypnotherapists who will guide them quickly and pleasantly to their solutions using this method. More details of the Association can be found at www.AfSFH.com.

This metaphor helps the client to understand the concept of solution focused thinking. Most clients will understand, and may have been previously frustrated by, the rules of searching for what they want on the internet using a search engine.

The language of successful internet searching has, for the vast majority, become second nature, and so by using this metaphor the client is able to begin understanding and learning the concept of putting the right criteria into their thoughts to illicit the right answer for their life.

As with other internet based metaphors, such as Facebook Timeline, this metaphor can also help to build rapport with younger clients and give them an explanation of solution focused thinking that they can relate to and easily understand.

The Big Book of Metaphors

The Big Book of Metaphors

Search Engine

GOOGLE BRAIN

Have you ever used Google to search for something you want or need on the Internet – or any other search engine for that matter? Where you typed in a word or phrase and it searches through all the information – millions and trillions of information and possibilities and provides the result for you – trawling for anything and everything that appears to match your words – faster than you can imagine bringing all the results it thought you wanted based on the words you used?

My friend was looking recently – at first she didn't really know what she was looking for – typing random words into the box – hitting search and hoping that she would be provided with something useful, something relevant, the answer to the question she wasn't really asking...

Of course, after a while she got fed up and despondent – the search engine wasn't finding anything she wanted or needed. She blamed the search engine, of course, felt it didn't work properly or was deliberately making things difficult for her; she even blamed the people behind Google, feeling they'd provided her with a programme designed to make sure she couldn't get what she wanted and needed – she got very angry at them and at herself – she even shut down the computer for a while – declaring it was useless, worthless, incapable and pointless –

After a while she began to realise where she'd gone wrong though – realising she'd not actually been clear enough about what she was looking for, so she decided to give it another go –

'No noise' she typed in – and the results popped up milliseconds later – one million websites about NOISE! 'Hmmpphhh!' she thought, that's not what I wanted; she tried again 'no problems' – 52 million sites of problems! 'Grrrrr!' this isn't working!! 'Tired all the time', another few million sites about being tired all the time – 'stressed', 'anxious', 'frustrated', 'lazy', 'lack of concentration' – billions and billions of sites showing all these things – not one of them what she was looking for or wanted – and you can imagine, the more she searched in this way, the more she became all of these things and the computer lid got slammed shut once again...

Days passed as she stewed on this and all the other problems, ever more convinced it was all impossible and there was no way forward;

until someone suggested a solution to her – quite literally – that gave her enough hope to try one more time –

'Peace, tranquillity, energy, motivation, calm, relaxed, harmonious, focused' were the words she typed in – and all of a sudden Google presented her with everything she wanted! And oh, how she enjoyed those websites!

Life is a bit like Google you know, if we keep typing in the problem, the result we get *is* the problem – whereas if we search for the solution we're all of a sudden being presented with all the information we could ever need or want about the solution! Choose your search criteria carefully – your brain *is* your very own Google!

The Big Book of Metaphors

9. Fears and Phobias

This metaphor was written primarily for use when working with clients presenting with fears and phobias, although as with all the metaphors, it can be used in many other sessions where the therapist considers it will 'speak' to the client and help them understand something or view their situation from a different angle.

Fears and phobias are a common complaint that clients approach a hypnotherapist for help with. Clients present with a huge range of fears and phobias from the common, such as fear of flying, spiders and heights, to the more unusual such as buttons, fluff, balloons and beards.

A fear can be developed over just about anything and it is not unusual for the client to have no real awareness of where the fear came from. In solution focused therapy it's unusual to go looking for the cause of the fear as it is not deemed necessary and is usually irrelevant. Various 'fast phobia' techniques are used; many of which have been developed from Neuro Linguistic Programming techniques (NLP). A particularly good method is the 'Rewind' technique where the client, in a relaxed state, imagines a TV screen and video player with themselves in charge of the remote control. The hypnotherapist then takes them through a series of fast forwarding and rewinding a film of their fear.

Fears can sometimes occur as a result of a traumatic incident, but are sometimes developed purely through imagining a 'worst case scenario' - remember, the mind cannot tell the difference between imagination and reality. Repeated worry or imagining of the fearful scene, either consciously or subconsciously will cause the mind to think the incident has really happened not just once, but over and over again. This imagining or worrying about the worst case scenario involving the subject of their fear causes feelings of anxiety to be triggered. Where the brain experiences increased anxiety it assumes imminent danger from the subject in question and so will encourage more and more focus to be placed on the subject to ensure that action is taken. This increased focus, where no action is necessary, because the object of fear is only being imagined, leads to higher and higher anxiety, triggering a panic response.

It is thought that some fears are inherited genetically from our ancestors and this theory accounts for the common fear of spiders and snakes where the person has only ever lived in a country where these animals are now harmless; or of the dark where being in a darkened room presents no danger for most in modern living. In primitive times however, living in a dark cave would have been good reason for the rise in anxiety!

Where danger is perceived, the brain 'shortcuts' past our usual rational and logical processes and sends the information directly to the amygdala, the 'fight/flight' centre of the brain, triggering an appropriate response, switching off the digestive system, releasing adrenalin and cortisol into the system and speeding up the heart in order to pump extra blood into the system. It shuts off the ability to process logical and rational thought and blind panic ensues. It is for this reason that as the client becomes consciously aware of the object of their fear, they are often already in the grip of the panic response and unable to control it. After all, if a sabre toothed lion were to appear it would be a good idea for the body to be primed for action instantaneously, rather than still preparing for the action as the intellect registers, assesses and plans what action to take. Clients are rarely aware of the thought process that has caused the panic, only of the panic itself.

By going through the fast forwarding and rewinding required in the 'Rewind' technique the client is replicating what the mind naturally does in REM (Rapid Eye Movement) sleep. It is processing the information through the limbic (survival) system so the client is able to process the emotions and regain intellectual control over the object of their irrational fear. This is then backed up with a 'Reframe' where the hypnotherapist asks the client to imagine themselves alongside the event or situation acting in a calm and relaxed manner when exposed to the stimulus. In this way, the mind is able to experience the event or situation without emotional response. The mind records and stores this information so that when the client next exposes themselves to the stimulus, the mind will automatically search for the information held on the subject and instead of accessing a file that indicates fear and panic are required, finds a file that suggests they are calm and relaxed.

This technique can also be used for any event the client is struggling to process naturally through the limbic system so that they can 'let go' of the emotion. For these events, however, it would not always be necessary, or appropriate, to carry out a 'Reframe'.

The idea of deleting and downloading a new film is familiar to many people and the client doesn't need to have a particularly good awareness of how an iPad or other tablet works to understand the metaphor, as long as you are sure the client is computer literate, the concept should be understood sufficiently well.

The content of the film being downloaded can be adapted to fit in more fully with the fear/phobia being worked on. When adapting for other fears it is important not to make the content of the new film too literal. For example, it probably wouldn't be a good idea to suggest the new film is Arachnophobia if the client's fear is of spiders! It would be more comfortable for the client if the new film were, for instance, about someone camping, or visiting an old house and the subconscious mind will fill in the blanks that these would likely be places they would normally avoid because of the potential for running into a spider.

By collecting information in the initial consultation or first session about how the client would like things to be once they no longer had the fear or phobia it should be easy to devise a simple film plot based on this positive outcome.

This metaphor can also be used where the client is overly focused on a more general problem to help them to understand, and subconsciously act on, the need to clear out the old to make way for the new. In this case the content of the film being deleted could be adapted to depict the problem they have presented or keep focusing on, so they can picture this being deleted. The new film is based on how they have said they would like things to be, so they can imagine this being a reality.

The Big Book of Metaphors

NEW FILM

I was thinking a few days ago about how great some aspects of modern science and technology are – I'm a big fan of gadgets, those little things that simplify my life and allow me to be much more productive and help me to enjoy my life a little bit more –

In particular I was thinking about my iPad. And I don't know how much you know about these things but it has the capacity to do so much, to hold so much information – I can do my work on it, I can access all sorts of information, listen to music – but one of the things I love to use it for is to watch films – and a few days ago I wanted to download a new film to watch on my tablet – it was a real 'feel good' film, it was a film about a family going off on holiday abroad – off to find sunshine and adventure in far off lands and I was so looking forward to watching this film – to enjoying their adventure with them, seeing the new sites and experiencing the new cultures and views along with them –

So you can imagine my disappointment when I found that the memory on my tablet was too full for me to download this new and exciting film – this film that was going to give me so much pleasure and open up a whole new world of experience for me – what was I to do?

Watching this new film, now that I knew it existed was something I really, really wanted to do….

So I decided if the memory were full, the only way forward would be to free up some memory by deleting an old film…..

So I looked through the films I had stored – there were some funny ones, some romantic ones, some dramas, some historical ones – all of which I wanted to keep – but then I noticed that there was a very scary film – a horror film I definitely did not want. The film made me feel bad, it made me feel frightened and frozen – it made my tummy churn and my heart race, and even after I'd finished watching it, it still haunted me, making me feel scared even when I wasn't watching the film – yes, I could definitely live without this film in my library – and so I made a decision; and as my hand reached out I was a little apprehensive as we tend to be when we do something so drastic on the computer – but I kept my nerve – DELETE – "are you sure?" it asked – oh yes, I thought – DELETE – and I watched as it went through that simple procedure of deleting the film I no longer wanted in my library – 30 seconds remaining, 20, then 10…..5, 4, 3, 2, 1 – gone!
And there – there was my space for my new film – a film that I could enjoy, one that I actually wanted in my library, one that was going to

make me feel good and add to my enjoyment, one that was going to allow me to learn about new experiences and adventures that were there to be had –

My hand reached out again – and with a sense of excitement and pleasure I clicked the button – DOWNLOAD NEW FILM – and watched that film being added to my library – the cover so lovely and colourful, the 'feel good' factor contained in it immediately obvious to me. "Would you like to watch this new film now?" my iPad asked me; "Yes I would" I replied very definitely – and it was everything I'd hoped it would be and more…..

And I wonder now how quickly you'll decide to watch your new film?......

The Big Book of Metaphors

10. Reticular Activating System

This metaphor encourages the client to understand how to bring positives in life into their line of vision.

Often a client will be having difficulties seeing the positives in life and become convinced this means they don't exist for them. This is because of the way the Reticular Activating System works.

The Reticular Activating System or RAS is the area of the brain responsible for filtering the six million pieces of information being presented to it each second of every day. The RAS filters information into what we need to be consciously aware of, and what can be ignored. Without the RAS it would be necessary for us to evaluate six million pieces of information a second. If this were even attempted it would leave us incredibly stressed, and wouldn't leave any time for doing anything else!

To help the client understand how the RAS works it is often a good idea to ask them to remember a time when they have been in a room full of people, all talking and being active when they suddenly become aware that they have heard their own name being mentioned. Most people have had this experience in their life at some point. It demonstrates perfectly that the client will not have consciously heard the content of the many conversations going on around them. The RAS will have filtered them out, but when their own name was mentioned the RAS decided it may be relevant for the client and so allowed it to be presented to their conscious awareness. The important fact here is that the RAS was aware of every single conversation that was happening as the subconscious sees and hears everything, even a pin dropping and it was choosing what to present to the client based on their current beliefs and thinking patterns.

The RAS takes its instructions from the conscious mind and passes it on to the subconscious. It then sorts through the subconscious and presents back to the conscious. For many clients, their RAS filter settings have, through their thoughts and behaviours, been set to look out for all the problems and difficulties in life, so the RAS is filtering out all the positives and only presenting the negatives to their conscious awareness. Where the client has focused their attention on the problem(s) for a period of time or consistently thought and stated their desires in a 'don't want' structure, the RAS has been misguidedly set to search and find every piece of evidence that matches what the client has focused on. It will always attempt to match any existing information pattern established in the mind and so it is important to consciously establish a new, more positive information pattern.

When clients are asked to detail what has gone well in their week they are consciously focusing on positives. This sends a strong message to the RAS to re-set the filters and begins looking out for positives and the required information pattern begins to build.

Until this new information pattern is established the RAS will continue to filter out much of this positive information. Because this process is happening on a subconscious level and only then being presented to the conscious part of the brain, the client will often struggle to present positives to the therapist. It is a great indicator to the therapist of how well the re-setting of the filters is progressing if the client is consistently asked about what's gone well in the time between each session. As the filter settings adjust, the client will be able to present more and more examples of positives to the therapist. A client should easily be able to state a minimum of ten positives about their week by the time they stop attending sessions.

Purple shoes are rare enough that the client will automatically recognise that sometimes you have to look a bit closer or harder to find what you want, but they are common enough for the client to be aware that they do exist.

Where the client or therapist is male this metaphor could be adapted, perhaps by renaming it 'Purple tie'.

There is a hidden bonus in this metaphor in that long after they have finished sessions every time they see purple shoes or ties they will reminded of the importance of looking out for the good things in life.

This metaphor can be used on or off the couch. When used in the talking part of a session clients will often adopt this metaphor as a way of saying they've had good things happen in the previous week. Asking a client what their 'Purple Shoes' have been during the week usually brings a smile and a more productive, positive answer when trying to illicit the good things that the client has noticed in between sessions.

The Big Book of Metaphors

PURPLE SHOES

If I were to ask you right now to tell me everything that had been good about your week, would you be able to? How many things would you be able to come up with that could go on the list?

Good things are like Purple Shoes……why? I hear you ask!!…..I'll tell you….

If I were to ask you right now whether you had seen any Purple Shoes because I wanted a pair and couldn't find any, it's likely you'd shake your head and say 'No, I never see Purple Shoes'

However….now that you know I'm looking for Purple Shoes I've brought them into your focus. You'd suddenly start seeing Purple Shoes on people walking by in the street, in the shops, on TV, you'd notice them if they were in the corner of the screen when you were surfing the net. You may even notice a pair of Purple Shoes peeking out from the back of your wardrobe that you forgot you bought so long ago.

As you started to become more aware of Purple Shoes, you'd start actively looking for them. In work you'd purposely look to see what shoes your colleagues were wearing. When your family came to visit you'd check out their shoes, when you were visiting the dentist you'd take a sneaky look just to check if there were any Purple Shoes there.

It would become a game you took pleasure from and maybe even a little sense of achievement each time you found a pair. You would start to realise there are Purple Shoes everywhere, then you would begin to congratulate yourself that you know this and that you know how to spot them and where the best places are to look. You may even return somewhere just because you know it's a place you've found Purple Shoes before and delight that there were more Purple Shoes when you got there.

Good things are like Purple Shoes.....

When you bring them into your focus and make yourself aware of them you suddenly realise they are everywhere. The more you find, the more you delight in them. The more you learn about where they are the more you visit that place.

Next time you think there's nothing good in your life, go looking for *your* Purple Shoes….you'll be amazed how many there are out there and where you'll find them.

The Big Book of Metaphors

11. Accepting Difficult Characters

Clients will often present saying that if this would change or that would change everything would be fine. The things they often want changed are not within their power to change and their resistance to accepting things, or people, as they are, leads to increased stress and anxiety. The mind then encourages them to focus more attention on these negative aspects because it perceives this as a problem that needs attention, in the same way it would if these aspects were an actual danger to the client. The Reticular Activating System (RAS) then begins its job of filtering out any other information as it begins to believe that the only aspect important to the client is the negative ones they are focusing on and the client begins to believe that the situation or person has no positive benefits or characteristics at all.

With increased focus on these negative attributes, the client experiences increased stress around this situation or person. Often, where the negative aspects are being perceived in a person the person is someone in the client's family, workplace or social circle and so their perception of family, work or social time becomes very negative.

Having a positive attitude towards these three main areas in life is essential for balanced mental health. Where a client is experiencing stress around one or more of these areas the overall balance will continue to suffer and resolution of the presenting problem becomes more difficult.

This metaphor reminds the client that whilst there are often aspects of situations or people they could do without, this is rarely the whole picture. It allows them to get a more balanced view and understand that what is being perceived as a negative could actually be a benefit when they look at the situation or person as a whole.

The metaphor is particularly useful where a client has a parent who is not as nurturing or gentle as they would hope, or who feels it is their duty to point out flaws in the client. A client can spend many years wishing their parent were different, or feeling a failure because the parent interacts with them in the way they do and this metaphor helps them to understand that's just the way they are and helps them accept the parent even with their 'lemon juice and salt' characteristics.

Many clients have a tendency to 'internalize' or to blame. They either feel they are somehow to blame for a situation or the way someone interacts with them or they absolve themselves of any responsibility at all and believe that the other person is wholly responsible for the problem or that they have no control over the situation at all.

Where internalization occurs the client develops an internal dialogue of worthlessness. Self-esteem and confidence suffer as a result and this can begin to cause problems in other areas of their life. Where blame occurs the client develops angry responses to thoughts and actual events that remind them of the unfair treatment. In both instances a 'victim' mentality can develop leading the client into more misery.

Solution focused questioning puts the client firmly back in the driving seat in these instances. A client who is thinking with the negative, emotional part of the brain will answer questions in a way that implies it is up to the other person to change. It is therefore important before starting this line of questioning to ensure that the client is in the intellectual, positive part of the brain.

This can be achieved by encouraging the client to talk about times they have done something that made them proud of themselves, or to recall a pleasant memory and describe it. As they re-create the memory the brain releases 'feel good' chemicals into their system and moves them away from the negative areas into the more positive areas.

Solution focused sessions tend to be happy, positive ones in the main because it is absolutely necessary for the client to be in this area of the brain to allow solutions to become clear.

When a client is in this positive frame of mind and is asked what they would need to be different in their life in order to move forward, they will come up with a more constructive reply than 'they [the other person] would need to change'. The focus of attention should always be on the client's behaviours and a more constructive answer would be along the theme of 'I would cope better'.

Where the client is adamant the other person needs to change it is fairly easy to direct their attention back to themselves by asking them what would be different for them if the person did change; what difference would others see in the client's behaviour if this person changed; how the client would feel differently if the behaviour changed, etc. This allows the client to start to see themselves in the way they would like to be. The intellectual mind will realise it is not actually necessary for the other person to change to allow the client to begin acting, interacting and thinking in the way they have described and will seek to help the client make their changes.

Hypnotherapist Michael Hughes*, who runs a successful practice and supervision group in Bristol developed a line of solution focused questioning whereby the client is asked to imagine that in the corner of the room there are five previous clients who had overcome the same problem currently being presented. He invites his clients to ask them questions about how they resolved their problems. They are then asked to suggest how they think these ex-clients would respond. This type of 'displacement' technique can help the client to see their problems and the possible solutions from a third party perspective. This creates for them the distance that is often necessary to see the 'whole picture'. This technique is particularly helpful where someone feels so 'stuck' in their situation that they have difficulty imagining themselves without the problem, while giving them an indication that this is not only possible, but a probable outcome.

This metaphor points out that sometimes there is lemon juice and salt, but that it is just a necessary part of the whole and should therefore be accepted. However, it also points out that they do have absolute control over what they choose to bring to the situation or relationship and therefore, thought about their role is necessary if there is any hope of a more positive outcome. There is no suggestion as to what their input should be, just some subtle suggestions of options.

*Michael is a fully qualified hypnotherapy supervisor. Supervision is a condition of membership with National Council of Hypnotherapists as well as other regulating bodies for newly qualified hypnotherapists. For more established hypnotherapists supervision may be optional. Please check your regulating body for rules and regulations regarding supervision.

Regular attendance at supervision, whether as a newly qualified hypnotherapist or the more experienced, provides excellent on-going support and also the opportunity to share knowledge and experiences. It also helps to keep hypnotherapists up-to-date with the latest research, techniques and available CPD courses.

To express an interest in joining Michael's supervision group please visit www.michael-hughes.co.uk

The Big Book of Metaphors

ROUGH PUFF PASTRY

I was thinking a couple of days ago about Rough Puff Pastry….just thinking about all the different things that can be made from this pastry….mostly I was thinking about cream horns and apple turnovers….I love to indulge in these wonderfully sweet treats every once in a while….sometimes as often as once a week, as long as I've been sensible about what else I do that week to ensure that I've kept the balance right….

What I found interesting though is the recipe for Rough Puff Pastry…..I wonder if you knew that sometimes it's made with salt and lemon juice?....now, if we eat either of these ingredients by themselves, they're horribly unpleasant; they make us feel bad, they're bitter and hard to swallow, they certainly aren't what we want out of a food, and we definitely wouldn't choose to eat them the way they are….

But when we mix them with all the other ingredients, something almost magical happens, those ingredients that are so unpleasant to us become essential to the finished product; they actually enhance the overall flavour….because of this we wouldn't want to change anything about these ingredients, we wouldn't want to make them sweet or warm, we wouldn't want their texture to become softer; in fact, we would be glad they are exactly what they are because they work so well with all the other ingredients and add the essential elements necessary for a perfect pastry....

And we do have the choice of what we add to that pastry to make it better; we could add a generous portion of something really sweet; or perhaps a sharp fruit – not too much, we wouldn't want to make it too sharp and we could smooth out that sharpness with a good dollop of comforting cream; or we may even decide sometimes to add something a bit savoury just to keep it all interesting....of course, whichever filling we decide to bring to the dish, the pastry stays just the same including its unpleasant ingredients that turned out to be so important, but the dish changes beyond recognition....so *we* get to choose what dish we prefer, and what we want to bring to the dish, while appreciating that *all* the ingredients made this dish what it is.....

I wonder which fillings you'd like to add to the dish?.....

12. Relationships and Neuroplasticity

This metaphor is for use with clients who have managed to extricate themselves from an unpleasant relationship only to then start viewing it through 'rose tinted glasses' and yearning to be back in the relationship. It is also useful for clients who are having difficulty moving forward after a relationship has been ended by the other person.

When someone begins a new relationship it is usual to spend time daydreaming about the happy future they are going to have with that person. Repeated daydreaming in this way encourages neural connections to be made in the mind so that everything to do with the new partner becomes 'linked in' to the images of the daydream. The beginning of a relationship and these positive daydreams activate a positive emotional reaction in the mind. When emotion is attached to thoughts, events and actions, the neural connections strengthen enormously.

This strengthening of the neural connections when strong emotion is experienced can be seen in evidence in the example of most people being unable to recall what they were doing on, for instance, Tuesday 28th August 2001, unless it was their birthday or some other special day for them. However, for the vast majority, recall for a date exactly two weeks later, on 11th September 2001, when the terrorist attacks happened in America, is crystal clear. Most people would be able to recall where they were, what they did that day and even how they felt as events unfolded. The emotional impact was so strong for so many people that the neural connections made during that 24 hour period were strengthened to the point that many of them are indelibly laid down in the mind. This process also happens where extreme positive emotions are experienced, for example at the beginning of the relationship which has ended for the client.

Because the mind cannot tell the different between imagination and reality, it behaves as if the daydreaming of the new relationship happened in real life. Where the relationship 'lives up to the dream' - even if only in part - these beliefs in the subconscious help support the relationship. The mind will filter information to support this pattern and allow the relationship to build and grow.

Where the reality does not match the dream in any way, and the person is consciously aware of this, the mind can start to filter information to support this negative belief. The relationship can then deteriorate to the point where one or both partners 'opt out' of the relationship. This can also happen where one or both partners have a strong negative belief subconsciously about themselves or relationships in general.

In some cases this can be confusing for the mind (and the client!). The current situation, created by conscious decisions, is in conflict with a vast file that indicates a fairy-tale romance in the subconscious. For some clients their subconscious belief in a romance gone sour over-rides the evidence of the problems there were in the relationship, creating an inability to 'let go' and move on.

Encouraging the building of new, positive neural pathways based on positive goals for the future without the partner, and focusing on positive action in the present, will reduce the strength of these old neural pathways. The brain works on a 'use it or lose it' basis where neural pathways are concerned. Where new, more positive pathways are built, the brain over time, comes to understand that the majority of pathways concerning the ex-partner are no longer needed and allows the neurons to be re-distributed; the emotional responses then reduce and disappear as the client moves forward into a brighter future.

This metaphor will remind the client there was a reason the relationship ended, whoever made the decision, and help them move on.

When dealing with relationship issues it is important that therapists stay aware that it is not within their remit to judge the value or otherwise of the relationship, but to help the client move forward in a way that is beneficial for them.

The Big Book of Metaphors

SOUR MILK

I heard a strange thing the other day – it quite surprised me and made me wonder….why? It was a very curious set of events that even now I'm having a little bit of a problem understanding…

A friend of a friend had some milk in his/her fridge – not so unusual I can imagine you're thinking – and it's not, not yet – the milk had turned sour though, so it was put in the bin – again, I can imagine you're thinking, that's not so strange; and of course, it isn't! It's what anyone would expect, if something's gone sour it gets thrown away, it's the sensible thing to do. If it doesn't go in the bin it just gets worse and worse; it becomes horribly unpleasant and can even start to affect all the other foods around it – then we find it's not only the milk that's sour but everything around it too; and that's even more horribly unpleasant than the sour milk could ever be. So we can see – the sour milk going in the bin isn't the strange part of this story – in fact, it's probably the most positive part of the story…

What is strange, what I had real trouble understanding – and I'm wondering if your powerful subconscious can help me with it – is this;

my friend of a friend wanted to go back to the bin and take the sour milk back out! He/she had this strange notion that, having spent some time in the bin the milk might once again be ok to drink! That if he/she could only retrieve the milk it may have lost its horrible smell and curdled appearance and have once again returned to the fresh, nutrient rich product it had been sold as in the beginning! It's very strange isn't it?

And what's even stranger is that my friend of a friend kept on going out to that bin to see if that milk was still sour instead of going to the shop to see if they had any fresh milk there…

It's all very strange isn't it? And doesn't seem to make much sense at all…

13. Planning To Achieve

This metaphor brings together all the necessary components for the client to make forward movement in their life and therefore become 'unstuck'. It is common for clients to approach a hypnotherapist because they have in some way become 'stuck' in a behaviour, situation or thought process and need help to find the way to begin moving forward again.

Where anxiety or depression is being experienced the mind will trigger the 'shut down' mechanism. This leaves the client with little or no motivation or planning skills to navigate around their problems, and reduces the chances of them exploring the idea of a better future.

When the amygdala, the fight/flight/freeze centre of the brain, is over-activated the effects are similar to that of an earthquake. With the amygdala at the epicentre, the tremors spread throughout the brain. It is often only when these ripples reach the pre-frontal cortex of the brain, or conscious awareness, that the client becomes aware and seeks help for the problems.

Because these tremors are being experienced throughout the brain there are many symptoms, some of which the client will not have related to their negative thinking or behaving. These tremors can affect their planning abilities, their concentration and their creative imagination.

Through sessions the amygdala's sensitivity is being reduced so the tremors become calmer and the client is able to proceed through life with these resources and abilities once again restored.

It is often the case during solution focused sessions that a 'top down' and 'bottom up' approach is being carried out. The solution focused questioning and goal planning in the first half of the session encourages the client to imagine their goals and plan how they will reach them, engaging their conscious faculties – the 'top down'. The second half of the session is given over to hypnosis, the 'bottom up'. By calming the amygdala and engaging the Anterior Cingulate (the secretary of the brain) the client is able work on how to make their goals possible.

The Anterior Cingulate is the best secretary you could ever imagine. It knows all the information that is stored in the subconscious and knows how to access it easily and quickly when we leave it to complete its work without interruption. It has the authority to over-ride other brain systems if it thinks the priority is high enough, is efficient and doesn't make a fuss while it carries out its duties. Unfortunately, for many the conscious part of the brain constantly interrupts the Anterior Cingulate in its work and frequently lets the Anterior Cingulate know that it doesn't trust it to carry out the task successfully. During trance the Anterior Cingulate is free to carry out its duties uninterrupted and the results can begin to be enjoyed by the client.

This metaphor reminds clients of the importance of imagining something different for themselves in a very real way, thus giving the job instructions to the Anterior Cingulate. Filling in the details of that picture increases their motivation to move towards their goals, thereby raising the priority of the job and letting the Anterior Cingulate know that it's ok, if necessary, to over-ride the other brain systems to achieve that goal.

It also reminds the client of the importance of planning how they are going to achieve their goals and that the journey can be a pleasure in itself.

The metaphor can be adapted to a tourist attraction in your area which is known but does not have a very obvious route to get there so that the client understands that effort is required to get to where they would like to be in life. However, it is not important that the client or therapist be knowledgeable about this tourist attraction as the meaning is in the planning and journey rather than the great ship docked in the West Country, UK.

The Big Book of Metaphors

SS GREAT BRITAIN

A friend of mine recently told me about her experience of trying to get to somewhere new and how she went about it.

She'd been aware of the historical ship, SS Great Britain all her life and how it was a great tourist attraction in her home country of Britain, and even better, was docked in her home city of Bristol.

On occasions through her life she'd found herself on the opposite side of the river that docked the great ship and would gaze across at the ship that so many others enjoyed and think she would quite like to get there one day. The problem is, she had no real sense of direction and there is no bridge from the side of the dock she was standing on to the side that the SS Great Britain is on to allow her to get there quickly and easily.

She realised not long ago that actually visiting the ship had not been a high enough priority for her to go to the trouble of finding the route to get there.

As she realised this she began to understand that if she knew more about the SS Great Britain and what it had to offer her if she were to make the effort to get there she might be more inclined to take the trouble to take the first steps necessary in the journey.

So she began to learn more about the ship and started to imagine how great it would be to walk the deck and feel the satisfaction of having finally got there. The picture became clearer and clearer in her mind as she started to fill in the details of how it would be to be in the ship and what the view would be like. She imagined how much her family would enjoy being there too. And as the picture became clearer so did her sense of excitement and through her research and imagining she realised it *was* somewhere she really, really wanted to go…that it would be worth the effort of finding out how she could do that.

So, she took out her map and planned her route. She planned to avoid as much traffic as she could so her journey would not be slowed too much, although realistically she knew she couldn't plan to avoid *every* hold up along the way. While she was planning she began to realise how many lovely places she would get to go through on the way and understood that she would enjoy the journey as much as she would reaching the destination. And she did!

I wonder where you'd like to go and if you can research your destination, plan your journey and imagine being in that place….right now, or sometime over the next week…

The Big Book of Metaphors

14. Pregnancy

Fertility and childbirth can be an extremely interesting and rewarding area of work for a hypnotherapist. The knowledge that the help that has been provided has enabled a human life to come into existence is truly amazing.

For some clients who have been through fertility and pregnancy difficulties previously, achieving their goal of becoming pregnant can lead to increased stress levels.

This metaphor has been written for clients who are in the early stages of pregnancy and are anxious that the pregnancy may end in a miscarriage.

Pregnancy may have been achieved where the client's reason for approaching a hypnotherapist is to become pregnant, or it may have been achieved as a by-product of receiving treatment for other difficulties.

When a client is suffering high anxiety the mind is reluctant to allow conception to happen. This can affect the client's hormone levels and menstrual cycle.

With fertility, pregnancy and childbirth issues it is always much easier to look towards the animal kingdom to understand and explain what the body is doing. Where an animal is in extreme danger, pregnancy is highly unlikely. The body activates mechanisms to ensure that conception does not happen to protect not only the prospective mother but also any danger the infant may encounter at birth. This is also true for human beings. It is rare in the Western world and in modern society for there to be the levels of danger referred to. However, the primitive areas of the mind responsible for reproduction are not aware of this. This is the area of the mind concerned with our survival and it has no intellect attached to it, so it is unable to 'think through' a situation. Its job is only to respond to the signals that are being sent to it.

Where a client is experiencing high anxiety (and it's true to say that almost all clients who seek help are experiencing an elevated level of anxiety) the mind is unable to establish what the cause is and so treats all anxiety as a signal that there is life-threatening danger in evidence. These levels of anxiety are sometimes chronic stress caused by modern living, the media, job demands, finances, family concerns, etc., or can be a result of more acute stress brought on by a particular event in the client's life. Whatever the cause of stress, it has been accompanied by re-current worrying, negative introspection about the past, negative forecasting about the future and/or complaining. All of these thinking patterns increase stress, contributing towards the mind's assessment that pregnancy is probably not the best idea.

This scenario can also create problems delivering the baby from the body. Again, if we turn to the animal kingdom we will see that an animal that is not in a safe environment will not go into labour. Furthermore, if labour has already begun and the animal is disturbed, labour will be slowed down or stopped to give the opportunity for the danger to pass or for the animal to move. In humans their worry about labour and birth, their resistance to labour and birth and their negative thinking about the process, is perceived by the mind as danger. The labour is not only delayed, slowed down or stopped, but the muscles also become tensed and ready to 'fight or flight', restricting the ability to contract the muscles in the uterus necessary for labour and delivery.

Sessions to help a prospective mother overcome their anxiety during pregnancy are as important, if not more important, than sessions given to help fertility or childbirth. The client may have many reasons - some valid - for fearing the premature end to their pregnancy and this metaphor is suitable no matter what the circumstances around conception are.

Where a client has been worrying about miscarriage they will have been subconsciously visualising this event happening. This metaphor redresses the balance by subtly encouraging a positive visualisation. The subconscious will 'pattern match' the sticky bud sticking to the chair and the embryo attaching to the uterus thereby creating the positive visualisation without the client feeling threatened by suggestions that they invest all their emotional resources into visualising the baby. For most clients in this situation, emotional investment of this level feels too much of a risk and is likely to increase anxiety at a time when calmness needs to be encouraged.

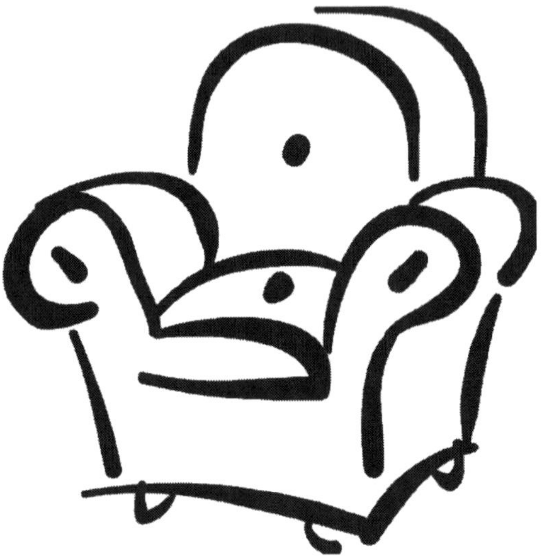

STICKY BUDS

I once saw a picture of a garden chair in a magazine. It was the loveliest garden chair. Rather than the usual slightly uncomfortable chairs I had always had this one was luxuriously comfortable – in fact it was more like an indoor armchair than a garden chair and it came attached to a gazebo to keep it dry.

If you can imagine this chair – it had a deep, comfortable seat and plump, plump cushions – designed for maximum comfort and support. There were wonderfully plump seat cushions; a big snug back cushion and even sumptuous arm cushions; I can't tell you how inviting that chair looked – I expect you can imagine though – soft and squishy, warm and inviting…

I decided a little while later that I just had to have a chair like this for myself. The first thing I had to do, of course, was to re-organise my garden so the chair would benefit from the best sunshine, the best views and maximum protection from the elements. Once that was done I went ahead and ordered my chair. I chose a rich, vibrant red material for it and could already imagine this wonderfully plump chair, so welcoming and pleasing.

I was aware, of course, that these things don't arrive as soon as we decide we want them, but I did my best to be patient while I waited, and in the meantime continued to improve my garden in any way I could to welcome my chair – seeing in my mind's eye – as I'm sure you can – that soft, red, plump chair...

And the day came when the chair arrived and I gazed at it so admiringly – it seemed just absolutely right that it should be in my garden, where it fit exactly where I'd wanted it...

A few days later I went to look at my chair and to my surprise – there attached to the arm of the chair was a sticky bud – you know the type you come across in fields, that get on your clothes and you can't move them? It seemed to be embedded into the pile of the material, stuck fast.

Now, I didn't want to remove this sticky bud, stuck so firmly with its hook like hairs – it was nestled so firmly I was reluctant to cause damage to the chair by doing that – so I let it stay there – where it seemed to nestle deeper and deeper into the very fibre of the chair, until it almost seemed to become a part of the chair itself – my deep, red, plush, plump chair; with the sticky bud firmly attached – held fast in the way that nature can design if the conditions are right – clinging on, day in, day out, nestling deeper and deeper into that fibre.

It didn't matter if I used the chair, moved the chair, or even turned that chair upside down. That sticky bud held fast. I had no idea if that sticky bud was blown in naturally on the wind or whether someone had put it there – and it didn't matter – all I know is, it had become a part of the chair and was there to stay. All I could wonder is whether this would be the only one, or whether more would appear in time; but that wasn't something to wonder about now; I could just accept the one that was here for now, stuck so fast in my perfect red chair that it had become a part of it...

15. Migraines

Migraines are thought to be caused by low levels of serotonin. As the levels drop the blood vessels in the brain constrict causing the 'aura' that many migraine sufferers experience. The blood vessels then widen and this causes the pain.

It is always worth stressing to the client that the actual brain does not feel pain; there are no pain receptors in the brain. It is the skin and muscles of the scalp that are feeling the pain. This distinction can be important to some clients experiencing migraine as they come to recognise that the pain is on the surface of their head, not inside it.

Hypnotherapy encourages the production of serotonin necessary to reduce or eradicate migraines. Positive thoughts, positive actions and positive interactions all contribute towards the increased levels of serotonin being created. Serotonin is the mind's natural reward system for carrying out behaviours necessary to ensure the survival of the species. This system of reward can be traced back throughout the history of man. When early man displayed behaviours that were necessary to survival such as hunting and gathering (exercise and work) and successful tribe living (positive social interaction) the mind produced high levels of serotonin that allowed intellectual control to be maintained. This contributed to the ability to cope with day to day living, acted as a motivator and encouraged more positive thoughts, actions and interactions. The brain still works in the same way today and deviation from these basic principles results in lowered levels of serotonin, thus creating physical symptoms such as migraine.

As the client regains intellectual control through the processes of goal setting, positive thinking and planning and increased awareness of what is going well, backed up by the dampening of amygdala activity created during hypnosis, they experience an increase of serotonin which in time leads to a decrease of the effects of migraine.

Where a client has been experiencing frequent, severe migraines over a period of time, they sometimes come to identify themselves as a migraine sufferer and the migraines become the focal point of their lives; restricting their activities and social interactions, leading to a further reduction of serotonin being released into the system, and therefore more migraines. They will often spend much time trying to identify foods, environments, physical and emotional 'triggers' for the migraines which leads to further focus being placed on the condition and the migraines begin to dominate their thoughts and lives.

Helping the client to identify what happens in the times they are <u>not</u> suffering from a migraine and building on these can help to shift the focus. This enables the client to begin to see that there are times when they are not suffering or their suffering is greatly reduced. This allows them to begin to plan to maximise the enjoyment of life in these times, rather than focusing all their attention on when the next migraine may occur or constantly looking out for signs that one is on its way. As the client begins to re-focus their attention, serotonin production increases and the spaces in between migraines begin to increase, leading to further releases of serotonin and so on.

It is often the case that when a client feels the first symptoms of a migraine, their stress levels increase in anticipation of the problem occurring helping to ensure that the feared migraine will appear.

In this metaphor the coloured flashes of lightning are used to signify the flashes of colour that some migraine sufferers experience. This can be adapted to suit the symptoms of particular clients as everyone experiences migraines in different ways. For instance, for a client who suffers from blurred or double vision you could include rainfall in the description of the storm which makes it difficult for [her] to see clearly; or have the sun just visible behind the thick heavy clouds creating blinding brightness on the horizon for clients who experience 'auras' as part of their symptomology.

The idea of having a palm sized remote control with which the symptoms can be turned down returns an element of control and empowerment to the client. The technique can be used by the client in between sessions as well as into the future. When a client focuses their attention in this way they are using their intellect to visualise and control the storm. Intellectual control leads to a more positive thinking pattern and precedes the production of the necessary serotonin.

Clients can be taught self-hypnosis to maximise the benefits of this metaphor when they are using it between sessions. A simple process of closing their eyes, slowing the breathing, focusing on the breath coming in and out of their nostrils and sinking into the most comfortable place they can imagine, feeling the calmness and relaxation enveloping them and visualising the park around them noticing the colours, the smells, the textures and the sounds, should be sufficient for the client to then take control of the storm. With practice this process becomes easier and easier for the client who should be encouraged to practice as frequently as is comfortable in the initial stages until the mind begins to recognise what is required of it when the eyes are closed and the breathing adjusted in this way.

It is said that the brain is able to establish new habits with consistent application within 30 days. This is how long it takes for the neurons in the brain to build up a new pathway. Each time the client practices the self-hypnosis, electrical impulses travel from neuron to neuron establishing new connections. The more often this is done the easier it is for the brain to fire the electrical impulses between the involved neurons. Through repeated firing along this pathway the connections become more solid and the neurons 'wire together'. Once they have wired together they begin to produce proteins that allow this pathway to be laid down in the long term memory and become a habit. For maximum results the client should be encouraged to carry out this exercise at least three times daily for a minimum of 30 days.

The Big Book of Metaphors

The Big Book of Metaphors

STORM CONTROL

And this story starts in the way so many do – with the words "Once Upon A Time" – and this is any time, in any place – and it's a very enlightening story and one that I think will be of great interest to you –

Once upon a time there was a girl. This girl was sitting in the middle of a park, in the bandstand – and she was waiting for her friends, looking forward to the fun they were going to have together – doing all the things she liked doing best, and just enjoying the time they would spend together, and the sense of freedom that this large park with the pretty coloured flowers and shrubs and trees gave her – I wonder if you can picture that park in your mind's eye – it may have been a park you've visited before, or it may be one that you create from your own imagination –

As she sat – enjoying the fresh air and the sound of birds singing in the trees around her she looked into the distance – and with a feeling of dismay saw the storm clouds gathering on the horizon – thick and black – angry looking clouds, moving ever closer – she felt her spirits plummet – knowing that they were going to ruin her day, maybe even the next couple of days – and she could sense already that all the fun she had planned for the next couple of days wasn't going to happen – her shoulders drooped, her good mood vanished, her thoughts turned dark – the quicker her mood descended the quicker the clouds moved towards her. The air thickened, and as the clouds drew closer she could begin to see the lightning on the surface of those big, black, heavy clouds – but this was no ordinary lightning, this was lightning of all different colours – crimson and royal blue lightning, vivid greens and yellows – mixing in with the white hot lightning – breaking through the air like angry spikes reaching down menacingly – and she could hear the thunder, roaring loudly – all of it coming closer and closer – closing in on her quicker and quicker until it was immediately over her – the storm all around her –

She curled herself into a ball, trying to shut out the storm, closed her eyes tightly against the lightning but it seemed to penetrate her eyelids with those angry flashes of colour – she had no idea how to get away from it – there was nowhere to run, nowhere to hide –

And then her eyes found an object on the floor of the bandstand and in her curiosity she reached forward to see what this object was – as her fingers closed around the cool object which fit neatly into the palm of her hand she realised it was some sort of remote control – this remote control had only one button – with arrows up and down. The girl pressed the up arrow – and as she pressed that button the storm became angrier – the clouds became darker and darker – the lightning more and more furious, the air became thicker and thicker, so thick she felt she couldn't even move as the storm closed in tighter and tighter around her, holding her tightly in its grip, tense and afraid, totally focused on the storm around her -

Quickly realising what had happened she pressed on the down arrow and as she pressed that button she noticed the air clearing, lightening, releasing its grip in her, freeing her – the lightning became less angry, less aggressive, less vivid and the clouds started to thin – she could see them moving apart – starting to drift again – she carried on pressing that "down" arrow and the angry colours of the lightning began to change, from crimson to a soft, baby pink – from royal blue to a gentle sky blue, the warming sun broke through, penetrating her skin and relaxing her; the thunder quietened and the sound of birds could be heard once again. The girl relaxed as the storm released. She opened her eyes and looked around her and could once again see the rich green of the grass; the vibrant colours of flowers; breathe the clean, pure air around her….and there in the distance were her friends and all was right in the world.

Finding the remote control is key….once it's found, operating the up and down button is the skill that can be learned – and the more we practice something the quicker we learn…

16. Strong Willed Clients

For some clients approaching a hypnotherapist for help with their problems is an incredibly difficult step. Their sense of frustration, feelings of failure and/or weakness and embarrassment at having to admit they have lost control has often contributed to the very problem they are seeking help for.

These clients are often those who have always been seen to be very strong; have spent much of their life helping others with their problems; or have been dismissive of other peoples' inability to cope. For these clients the symptoms they are experiencing can have shaken their core belief system about who they are.

They are confused about how they've become someone who needs to seek help and can be angry or resentful at this state of affairs. They may even display signs of contempt towards the very person they have approached for help, and can be slightly dismissive of the process. They behave as if they are doing the hypnotherapist a favour by attending the sessions and don't really need the help but are going to keep attending anyway. They will sometimes attempt to 'control' the session as a coping mechanism.

For the hypnotherapist this can be very disconcerting and can sometimes shake the confidence of the therapist. It is important to recognise that these behaviours are a result of the client's own difficulties in admitting they have not been able to cope and not a personal attack on the hypnotherapist's abilities, knowledge or working practices.

It is often helpful for these clients to understand that the act of approaching someone for help is a sign of control and courage. Although some clients will not value this information while they are in the initial stages of sessions, once they begin to regain intellectual control they will accept this logic.

For brain based hypnotherapists an initial consultation includes a discussion about how the mind works. This is usually broken down into information about the intellectual area of the mind and its ability to think things through in a logical, rational way versus the survival area of the brain which behaves within the parameters of fight, flight or freeze actions. This explanation will alert these clients to the fact that they have been operating within the parameters of the primitive mind without too much emphasis having to be made. However, strong emphasis should be placed on the client's retention of intellectual control which has allowed them to identify that there is a problem and led them to seek out help and attend the sessions. Any other examples the client has disclosed that indicate intellectual control should also be emphasised. This should help the client's attitude towards the hypnotherapist and enable the sessions to become more positive as they receive acknowledgement of their strengths and indications that they are in control.

Solution focused work is often welcomed by these clients. When the discussion being held is of a solution focused nature, the therapist is acknowledging the client as the expert. The therapist's questions must always come from a place of 'not knowing' and be curious in their delivery.

Carl Rogers, the psychologist who founded person centred therapy, believed that all clients already have all the internal resources necessary to overcome their difficulties. He considered that by displaying unconditional positive regard, clients are able to access all the solutions necessary to resolve their problems. Solution focused questioning, with its 'not knowing' nature delivers this unconditional positive regard. When therapist's questions are coming from a place of 'not knowing' they are without judgement or expectation of an answer based on their own view of the world. They acknowledge and respect that the client has his or her own view of the world and that solutions will need to fit with the clients own belief system.

Clients who are used to being in control will be pleasantly surprised and reassured that the therapist is not going to try to take control or tell them what they must do, but are allowing them space to make their own decisions on what needs to be done to move forward.

This metaphor is a useful way for the client to understand why they are not coping with life especially if they feel they should be able to or are confused that there have not been any identifiable reasons for them to have run into problems.

It is often a build-up of thoughts, behaviours or events that have led the client into their symptoms rather than any major life events. For many clients just understanding how everything has managed to get on top of them will be a big help in allowing them to let go of the stress and anxiety of trying to work out why they feel like they do or being embarrassed because they feel they should be able to cope. Once the client is freed from focusing on the why, they can begin to focus their attention on how they want to move forward.

Many people are familiar with the computer game Tetris where different formations of squares fall from the top of the screen and have to be turned in the correct way to fit together once they reach the bottom of the screen without leaving any gaps. Anyone who has ever played the game will be familiar with the sense of panic and/or defeat as you realise the game is throwing more challenges at you than you can respond correctly to and how this can quickly and easily lead to losing control.

The Big Book of Metaphors

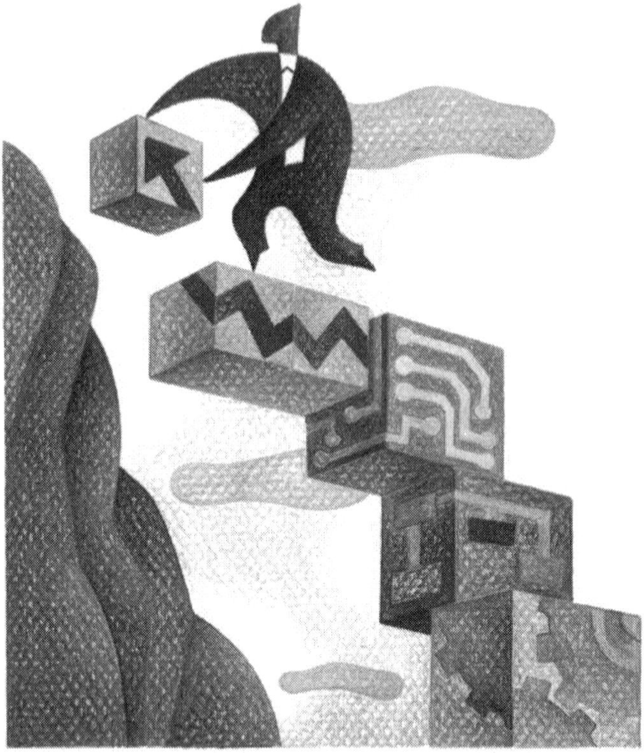

TETRIS

It's a little like a game of Tetris. The shapes come down and they all fit together perfectly and the game is easy, when everything fits together the part that's completed just disappears – the achievement barely noticed or recognised; certainly not acknowledged, it just vanishes off the screen, almost an expected result and everything just carries on smoothly...

But then a block falls the wrong way, you almost didn't even notice it coming until it created a problem that shouldn't be there – it's upset the balance and you focus entirely on it and start reacting to that misplaced block and the more you focus on this mistake the more you miss what else is happening on the screen and you suddenly realise there's another problem, and another and another...

The blocks seem to start falling quicker and quicker, quicker than you can perhaps deal with and it becomes more and more difficult to deal with them as there's less and less room to move and the whole thing builds up and up while you panic and stress – no coherent thought as everything seems to run out of control and still you try to deal with the blocks that keep coming, finding it ever more difficult to place them in their perfect order and fit everything together in that easy and satisfying way – and then the disappointment as you begin to admit defeat and the game begins to win…

But you can play again – learning the lessons, coming up with a new game plan – a couple of deep calming breaths as the blocks start coming again –

This time you're calm and in control; you're pleased with yourself each time you complete a row successfully; aware of the achievement, pleased that you're doing so well. Then the first problem occurs; but when it doesn't all fit together perfectly in the way you'd hoped you keep a cool head and re-assess what you're now working with; accepting the error and moving on swiftly; remembering to maintain focus on the ultimate goal – to only create as many perfectly aligned blocks as you can; so you forget the problem one and move on to making the next line perfect, and the next and the next as the problem sinks down the screen into insignificance – a minor blip and there's still everything to play for. You keep your focus, you accept what's happened and move on quickly, and the more often you do it the easier it becomes…

And when you move up to the next level, you see the screen wiped clean and you start again with a clear screen – those problems you made sure were minor problems by the way you dealt with them are the parts that disappear – the problem barely noticed or recognised, and certainly not the focus – while you keep your full attention on the achievements as everything begins to fit together again in the way it can – and the achievements get greater and greater as you play the game -

The Big Book of Metaphors

17. Anxiety and Panic Attacks

This metaphor is particularly useful for clients experiencing high anxiety. It is often the case with these clients that they are unaware of their thought processes but are very aware of the physical responses these induce. They often state that it is the feelings, such as churning tummy, restlessness, sweaty palms, etc. that make them think in a negative or anxious way rather than the negative thoughts, worries or anxieties <u>creating</u> the feelings. It is also not unusual for a client struggling in this way to state that they awake in the morning with these symptoms and this then dictates to them that they will have a "bad day".

It is useful to make the client aware of 7/11 breathing to reduce the symptoms of anxiety. 7/11 is the act of breathing in for the count of 7 and breathing out for a count of 11. When clients breathe in this way the parasympathetic nervous system is stimulated. The sympathetic nervous system activates the fight/flight mechanism which will bring about the symptoms of anxiety described above. The parasympathetic nervous system is the opposing system responsible for rest and relaxation. It is not possible for both these systems to be active at the same time.

When the parasympathetic nervous system is activated muscle relaxation occurs, heart rate slows, the digestive system is stimulated (reducing the 'churning effect'), the brain activity alters to cognitive functions and the intellect is engaged. Encouraging counting as the client undertakes the breathing allows them to focus their attention away from 'problem' thoughts.

For optimum effect, abdominal breathing is advised. This is the act of breathing with the tummy, so that the tummy rises and falls, rather than the chest. Many people struggle to achieve abdominal breathing in the initial stages as they are used to taking more shallow breaths originating in the chest area. When the client lies flat on their back abdominal breathing is automatic. This can give the client the opportunity to experience this type of breathing with little effort and with practice this becomes easier to do when sitting or standing.

Increased control of the symptoms of anxiety can help the client towards a feeling of control. However, it is important to focus attention on the root cause of the anxious feelings or panic attacks that the client is experiencing.

The client may have experienced a previous traumatic incident that is contributing towards their anxiety or panic attacks and these can be helped using the Rewind technique referred to in Chapter 9. However, it will also be necessary to focus the client's attention on improving their overall thought process to bring about long term change reducing opportunity for a recurrence of the problems.

Clients are often unaware of how their general thought process and outlook on life has contributed to, or caused, the problem of anxiety and panic attacks. It can be a very gradual build-up of negative thinking that has caused the symptoms they are now struggling with.

Where this is the case the client may not be aware that their thought processes and internal dialogue have changed.

It is often believed that thinking and imagining negatively is a harmless pastime. A client may regularly spend time thinking uncharitably about another person or a situation and take some joy in imagining how they would like to deal with the person or situation in an unpleasant way. They may feel justified in telling others about what a terrible place the world is and how modern society, teenagers, social media and technology and the programmes on TV are all awful and it is these things that have created all the problems in the world today. They may be plagued with negative thoughts about themselves, for example, constantly thinking how horrible their hair is; or wrinkles; or body. It may be that they constantly complain about their partner children, parents or siblings. They often use the word 'but' or phrases such as 'the trouble is...' Sometimes inordinate amounts of time are spent thinking and talking about how much they hate their job; worry over finances; replaying events of their childhood or difficult events of their adult life, or perhaps worrying about their health, age, property or abilities. These are all examples of what is meant by 'negative thinking'.

Clients will often be adamant that they are not negative and this is usually because they do not fully understand what is meant by negative thinking. It is quite often the case too that the negative thinking has become such a habit, the client is not consciously aware of it. The language patterns used by the client when they are talking are usually a good indication of their thought processes.

In Dr David Hamilton's CD 'Secrets & Rules for Attracting What you Want', a recording of a live lecture, he speaks of a young man who kept a 'Gratitude Diary' where he wrote down each day everything he was grateful for. This had a huge effect on his life and altered his thinking patterns to focus on the positive aspects of life. This can be a useful suggestion to make to the client who is struggling to grasp the understanding or technique of positive thinking. For information about this CD please visit www.drdavidhamilton.com.

By working with the feelings of anxiety as well as the cause of those feelings, the client is able to make forward movement and feel empowered to control their own symptoms.

This metaphor allows the client to imagine waking up in the morning and finding that they are calm and relaxed and will encourage them to imagine how the day will progress on a 'good day', thereby encouraging this into reality.

The client can be encouraged to use this metaphor along with breathing exercises to induce calmness wherever necessary. It will also be a useful line of solution focused questioning as it allows the client to express what would be different about their day if the feelings were not there. This helps them to build a positive picture so they can begin behaving in this way despite the feeling they've woken up with and encourage a positive thought process. This will naturally lead to the feelings reducing or disappearing during the day and create a much higher chance of them being absent the following morning. It is important for a client to understand that it is the thoughts and actions of the previous day or days that lead to the feeling being in evidence upon waking and therefore labelling a day as a 'bad day' because the feeling is present upon waking will lead to a higher likelihood of the feeling being present again the following day.

The metaphor also encourages feelings of joy, happiness and positivity which will also help the overall problem.

The Big Book of Metaphors

THE GIFT

Someone I know recently received a gift – I don't remember which day she got it, I think perhaps it was a Thursday – I do know it was a special gift, whichever day it was she received it.

She didn't know she was going to get this gift, although she'd been hoping for it for a long, long time – without even knowing what she was hoping to get – and she didn't know when it arrived – it was just suddenly there in front of her when she woke one morning – big and shiny and wrapped with a bow, she didn't say what colour the paper was, or the bow, the paper may have been purple or green, or maybe blue or pink – whatever colour it was, it was most pleasing to her eye – the bow may have been red or perhaps silver – it complimented the gift perfectly – and I'm sure you know what colours they were….

When she opened the gift she didn't know at first that she was already receiving the gift as she untied the bow and carefully tore the paper away, when she carefully opened the lid she didn't know the gift had already started to escape; she only knew how she felt –

And she wasn't surprised that as the lid came off and she *saw* nothing because she already knew what she'd already known all along; that this was the most precious gift of all – and she *felt* the gift, and she *thought* the gift – and I wonder if you can feel and think that gift too – because this is *your* story and *your* gift – it's the gift of relaxation and calmness and peace of mind, it is the gift of happiness and control; it is the gift of positivity and joy – and I wonder how well you can feel and think this gift now, you can let yourself think and feel this gift – because this is *yours* now – it's become a part of who you are – others can see so well what a special gift you were given and how well you wear that gift and it's all yours now, you own it – and when we're given a gift like this we accept it gratefully and graciously, knowing that we are deserving of this great gift that we can appreciate today, tomorrow and every day for the rest of our lives – and you **will** accept this gift of relaxation and calmness and happiness, will you not?

18. Irritable Bowel Syndrome

This is a great metaphor for those suffering with Irritable Bowel Syndrome.

The fear of losing control of bowel movements often leads to increased anxiety resulting in increased 'looseness' leading to more fear and anxiety with the client finding themselves stuck in a negative 'loop' where it is the fear that creates the symptoms and the symptoms create the fear.

The National Institute of Clinical Excellence (NICE) who advise GPs on recommended treatments for illnesses, have acknowledged the role of hypnotherapy in the successful treatment of Irritable Bowel Syndrome and may advise clients to seek treatment of this nature where medication or diet advice has failed or been of limited success.

Hypnotherapists recognise that stress is the main contributory factor in IBS. The client may not be consciously aware that they are experiencing high stress as they are so used to living with this stress it has become 'normal' for them. However, the body is responding to this increased level of stress by displaying the symptoms of IBS.

When the Sympathetic Nervous System (the survival mechanism) is triggered it affects the digestive system leading to blood being diverted away from the gastro-intestinal tract and constriction of the intestinal sphincters. The blood is diverted away from the digestive system and into the arms and legs so that they are ready for 'fight or flight', leaving the digestive system deficient in energy and therefore unable to function in the usual way. The secretion of fluid is also affected which could account for the symptoms of diarrhoea many sufferers experience.

The parasympathetic nervous system aids digestion and so in this calm and relaxed mode it is able to operate in the optimum way and the symptoms are alleviated.

The survival area of the brain that triggers these responses does not understand why the stress levels are increased, or recognise a gradual rise in stress as opposed to a sharp rise. It only recognises that the level of stress has reached the 'trigger' point and steps in. It is unconcerned as to whether the stress is caused by the appearance of a sabre tooth lion, or the arrival of an unwelcome bank statement, for instance. It sends the same response regardless.

If it was the sabre tooth lion that had appeared it would not be a surprise that the body was expelling all its contents! If it were then necessary to hide out from that sabre tooth lion it would be incredibly dangerous to have to leave the hiding place and find a toilet when the urge presented itself!

This seems logical in the face of this type of stress. The body would act in such a way that ensures 'toilet duties' are taken care of quickly and easily and that they are not going to need to be repeated for a substantial amount of time.

The chronic stress experienced by the IBS client will not have the high peaks and troughs that occur when the lion presents itself; likewise, the toilet habits of the IBS sufferer replicate this situation but at a more chronic level.

The hypnotherapist will seek to reduce the client's stress levels to reduce the symptomology by focusing their attention away from the symptoms. In doing this, the client can begin to identify when the symptoms are reduced or absent so that they can make the choice to repeat or expand upon those behaviours that improve the problem.

Each client will have varying symptomology as the condition is thought to have little or no physical cause. Their worry about this symptomology will no doubt be increasing their levels of overall stress and may even be impacting on their ability to have the necessary positive action, positive interaction and positive thoughts about self that are necessary to counteract the stress levels and begin producing the necessary serotonin levels. These increased levels of serotonin help keep the client in intellectual control and thereby stimulate activation of the parasympathetic nervous system that aids digestion in the optimum fashion.

This metaphor has been written to address the fear of losing control where loose bowels are the client's primary concern. However, it can be adapted to address a reluctance to 'let go' by putting emphasis on visualisations of the lock gates being opened rather than closed, to allow the river to run freely again.

By using this metaphor the client is being given a sense of control and the subconscious is receiving the suggestion that it must control the movement, allowing the client to focus their attention away from the symptoms. It helps to overcome the problem that symptoms cause thoughts; and thoughts cause symptoms. This metaphor helps to ensure a positive attitude begins to build resulting in reduced physical action by the body.

The Big Book of Metaphors

The Big Book of Metaphors

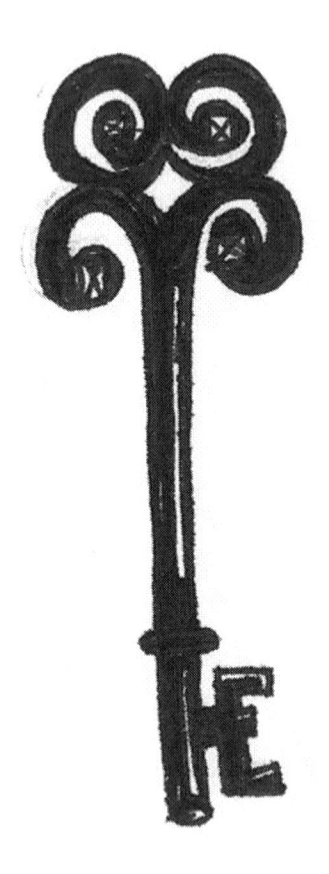

THE LOCK KEEPER

I had a friend who used to live next to a river and that river was a strong and powerful river – she remembers as a child constantly being told to keep away from it and she obeyed – it was so strong and uncontrollable she was more than happy to do what she was told...

There was a marina there too – lots of boats moored there...and it was so nice, to see those boats moored along their pontoons, clinging all along. So many of them, and sometimes it seemed as if the water had to squeeze through those boats – it would tug at them as it moved past, pulling and pushing them, activating them as it moved past, bringing them to life – sometimes she'd imagine they were annoyed with the water and were pushing back angrily at the water...

What fascinated her most though, was the lock. It fascinated her that those gates were so easy to move into place. Now I don't know how much you know about how locks work – but you have to stop briefly, put the key in the mechanism and turn the cog; it doesn't take long and those gates easily and quickly come together creating a barrier for the strong, fast flowing river – they close smoothly and easily, stopping that river in its tracks...no matter how much the river pushes against them they are secure, they make sure absolutely nothing is getting past them until the time and the circumstances are absolutely right to open those gates when you decide they need to be opened...

I wonder if you can see those lock gates now in your mind's eye – moving quickly into place – holding back the river – easily comfortably and with a strength you forgot was there – securing that river – it's all under control, your control – I wonder if, in fact, you can actually feel those lock gates closing now, closing tight until the right time to open them up again –

And I wonder if you know that you are the Lock Keeper...it's all in your control...

19. The Miracle Question

When using this metaphor it is a good idea to have discussed goals with the client immediately before they go on the couch so that the picture is at the forefront of their mind.

The Miracle Question devised by solution focused brief therapist Insoo Kim Berg of the Brief Family Therapy Centre in Milwaukee is a very effective way of building these goals.

In the Miracle Question clients are asked to imagine that they go to sleep as usual that evening and in the middle of the night a miracle happens which takes away the problem they are presenting with. The client is invited to explore what would be different when they awoke; how they would know the miracle had occurred; who else would notice and various other solution focused questions. This allows the client to suspend reality for a while and begin to think about how they would like things to be without being restricted by the idea of whether they think this is possible. It allows the focus of attention to be on the solution rather than the problem and can enable the client to become aware that some of this miracle may already be in evidence or can be easily achieved. This is very empowering for the client and allows them the feeling of being in control of their improvements. More information on the Miracle Question and Brief Family Therapy Centre can be found at http://www.sfbta.org/BFTC/Steve_de_Shazer_Insoo_Kim_Burg.html.

In this metaphor clients are encouraged to put events on a timeline and then float above this timeline, moving around it freely to allow the client to begin seeing the 'big picture' rather than focusing on the problem.

It is a good idea to leave quite a lengthy pause at the end of this metaphor to allow their subconscious to process everything they have seen or are experiencing. It can be quite difficult as a hypnotherapist to allow these long silences; it may even feel quite uncomfortable, however it is important to allow the client this time to process and become aware of their own solutions while the conscious mind is not interfering or judging the possibilities. Watching the second hand on a clock can help the therapist gain perspective on how long a silence is; what may feel to the therapist like forever is often only 30-60 seconds and this is a good length of pause to use.

No matter how uncomfortable the silence is for the therapist, remember the client is busy while on the couch and will be experiencing time distortion; in trance the client is neither focused on, nor paying attention to, the silence.

The pause given to clients is often the moment of greatest intuition, clarity and resolution and should therefore be utilized to the fullest; the client will always be glad of this opportunity to process.

The Big Book of Metaphors

The Big Book of Metaphors

TIMELINE

And I'd like you to wave your magic wand now and create the picture of you doing that which you have chosen to aim for…… allow the picture to build; to become clearer; see the detail; feel the feelings of being in that picture…..and I'll be quiet for a moment to allow you to create your picture in as much detail as is right for you…..

And I wonder if you can allow yourself to float up, higher and higher, so that you're above your picture, looking down…..seeing yourself in the scene….and I wonder if you can float a little bit higher now…. And when you look down you see that your picture has become a part of your very own time line, so that when you look into the distance you can see yourself right now, lying on this couch, listening to the sound of my voice…..

As you look at this timeline I wonder if you can see what you did to achieve your goal? How you got there? You may be able to pick out one or two scenes…..maybe more….that you see now really helped you to get to your goal….float downwards to take a closer look if you need to see in more detail those actions which helped you to achieve your goal……..

You may like to move further back from today…..you may spot something in the past that you did before today that you feel could help you again……this is your timeline….you can move freely up and down this timeline…….any time you feel stuck and are not sure which is the way forward you can move up your timeline to your goal and then float above to look back and see how you got to your goal……..and you may find some surprising steps there……that your conscious mind hadn't thought of yet……but your subconscious knew all along how to achieve that which you made a priority to achieve……..because we know that when you set your mind on a goal your solution focused subconscious will find imaginative ways to achieve that goal……when we just relax and allow the subconscious to guide us……..so I'll be quiet again for a moment while you float around your timeline……..moving in any direction you choose, to see what you need to see, to achieve that which you have clearly stated you want to achieve……….

20. Letting Go of a Relationship

The primary function of this metaphor is for clients who are struggling to let go of a relationship or ex-partner to move on. However, as with all other metaphors it can be used for any purpose you feel it would be suitable for. As previously stated, the gender of the story can be changed when being used for a male client.

When many people come to the end of a relationship they will spend time sifting through the details of that relationship, turning things this way and that in an effort to understand where it all went wrong. This is not unusual behaviour, and it can be useful to have a period of reflection so that valuable lessons can be extracted and used to the client's benefit in future relationships.

The beginning of a relationship is generally a time of optimum brain activity. When someone is experiencing the 'honeymoon period' they will often have a great deal of conscious awareness. The way they dress and present themselves, the way they behave and respond is something they give a great deal of conscious thought to, in an effort to present their 'best selves' to their new partner. Negative thought processes and habits are subdued and they become the person they would like to be seen as. They live very much 'in the here and now' because the 'here and now' is so pleasant and they are usually very active, social and positive.

The world becomes a much more pleasant place to be and their happiness is often tangible and contagious. Their mirror neurons are reflecting out the inner joy and excitement they feel and the world picks this up with their mirror neurons and reflects it back to them.

They rarely feel tired or get sick; they forgive others for actions that would normally drive them into irritation (including, perhaps, the new partner's actions) and are kind, patient and understanding.

Their thought processes are predominantly from the intellectual area of the brain and this leads to increased oxytocin (the 'love' chemical), the pre-cursor to the production of serotonin. The habitual area of the brain that usually leads them to act and think without conscious awareness is put to rest while they enjoy getting to know their new partner and everything is good.

Unfortunately, for some, relationships do not survive. The habitual mind steps back in, bringing with it the negative viewpoint; insecurities and doubts may surface; envy, impatience or anger may show themselves in one or both partners; the relationship loses its shine and eventually one or the other partner may decide that it's time to move on and look for the wonderful feelings they once had with another partner, or to at least give themselves that chance.

Quite often when the relationship gets to this point, for whatever reason it came to that point, one partner struggles to come to terms with the fact that what once felt like a dream has now turned to such sadness. They may possibly have sunk into depression and inertia takes over as their thoughts are frequently focused on the lost relationship.

For some clients this becomes a habit of thought and stops serving any purpose. This habitual thinking restricts the client from being able to notice and appreciate the life they have around them and to move forward. The more the client engages in this habitual thinking the more miserable they become; the more miserable they become the more they engage in the thinking and further re-enforce the habit.

It is often the case that through these habitual thinking patterns the view of the relationship becomes distorted. It is also frequently true to say that it is not, by this point any genuine emotional attachment to the ex-partner that is causing the upset but the self-imposed restriction the person has placed on their own life by spending so much time feeding this habit of thought.

This metaphor will help the client recognise that it's time to clear away the dead plants, accepting they've had everything good they were ever going to get from the relationship and start looking around for all the other opportunities there are to enjoy life; and perhaps become aware of someone else to build a relationship with, if that is their wish.

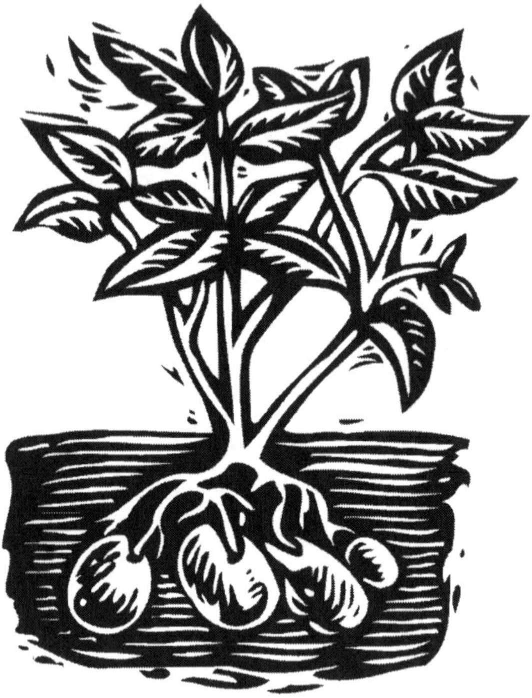

VEGETABLE GARDEN

My friend Rachel grew vegetables in her garden last year. It filled her with a real sense of pleasure to nurture these vegetables, to watch them grow and to imagine the rich abundance of food she was going to enjoy at the end.

In June she dug up the potatoes. She pulled the plants from the ground and picked off the potatoes attached to them and then she sifted through the ground to find any left there. Once she had collected all the potatoes she set the plants to one side on the ground….and left them there.

A couple of weeks later another friend visited Rachel and noticed that these old plants were still lying on the ground and asked Rachel why. 'I just want to study them for a while', she said, 'learn how they grew and remember all the details. I want to remember exactly how they were and see if I can identify how they could have been better or lasted longer'.

A few weeks later the plants were still lying on the ground, becoming increasingly unsightly now. 'Why', said Rachel's friend, 'are the dead plants still there?'
'Well', Rachel replied, 'I've become quite fond of looking at the leaves and the stalks and remembering how great they looked in the ground, and the good feeling it gave me when they were growing. I've become really interested in those old plants and don't really want to move them'.

The friend was quite confused by this, but chose not to say anything. She had seen the other vegetables were becoming ready to harvest and assumed that Rachel's attention would soon be taken up with these and she would forget about those old plants and finally throw them away.

The summer wore on and Rachel continued to focus her attention on those old, dead plants even though they were useless now and ugly. She sifted through them to see if she'd missed seeing anything that she hadn't noticed before. She thought about how many potatoes had grown on the plants and how she could have encouraged a greater crop and berated herself for not taking better care of them to allow them to grow more and more.

So focused was Rachel on these old dead plants that she failed to notice the peas ripening, or the tomatoes turning a bright, vibrant red, or even to notice the succulent strawberries that had swelled to perfection. As these other plants went unnoticed so the fruit dropped off and fell to the grown, wasted, uneaten and rotted where they lay. Each time Rachel looked out into the garden to look at her old potato plants she felt a sense of loss and misery envelope her and didn't understand why. She knew she wanted to keep those plants, that there was more to learn from them because she felt almost sure by now that there would never, ever be the chance to grow potatoes again. Eventually the whole garden looked like those old potato plants; dried up, empty and without a purpose. And still Rachel continued to look out into the garden, by now not even sure why she was doing it or what she was looking for.

It wasn't until the following spring when those other plants, the peas and tomatoes and strawberries that had not been dug up, just neglected terribly, began to grow again and produce beautiful flowers that filled the garden with pleasure again and the promise of food to come that Rachel realised that she had sacrificed all the wonderful offerings her garden had the previous year, just to focus on those old plants when all along she should have learned from the mistakes she felt she had made, planted new potatoes and enjoyed the experience of a new crop, as well as all the other fruits and vegetables she had and she resolved never again to let a single vegetable in her garden go to waste.

Rachel makes sure now that every time she looks at her garden she is looking at something bright and beautiful and worth looking at……..

Conclusion

The creative imagination is one of the most valuable resources we, as human beings, have at our disposal. This resource has served us for millions of years through evolution and has allowed us to move from primitive beings living in caves to the modern version of humanity. This ability to imagine a better future is what sets us apart from any other living species.

Metaphor allows us to ignite this valuable resource in our clients so that they may imagine a better future for themselves and resolve their problems in a safe, pleasant way.

It is said that the primitive, survival mind has the emotional age of a seven year old. All seven year olds respond to stories and these types of stories, with meanings hidden in the entertaining nature of the story have been used throughout the ages to pass on wisdom, aid understanding and unlock the naturally resisting nature of the mind to new ways of thinking and doing things.

I hope this book has ignited your own creative imagination and that these metaphors will become a valuable asset in your therapy toolkit to be enjoyed and interpreted by your clients to help them move into an era of greater happiness, activity and fulfilment.

Printed in Poland
by Amazon Fulfillment
Poland Sp. z o.o., Wrocław